SELL YOUR HOME

The complete Irish guide

to give your home that winning edge!

Con Nagle has always had an interest in property and, from a young age, attended many show houses with his father, Dick, a former President of the Institute of Professional Auctioneers and Valuers (IPAV).

After university, Con spent a number of years working for one of Ireland's main financial institutions before becoming an estate agent. He is now a director of Global Properties Ltd, Cork's largest estate agents, which has offices in Cork city, Ballincollig and Mallow.

Con is one of only a handful of estate agents who are members of both auctioneering bodies in Ireland: the IPAV and the Irish Auctioneers and Valuers Institute (IAVI). He has a master's degree in economics, from University College Cork, and is married to Maria, a Kilkenny native. They and their three children live in Ovens, just outside Cork city.

SELLING YOUR HOME

The complete Irish guide

to give your home that winning edge!

Con Nagle

THE O'BRIEN PRESS
DUBLIN

First published 2007 by The O'Brien Press Ltd,
12 Terenure Road East, Rathgar, Dublin 6, Ireland.
Tel: +353 1 4923333; Fax: +353 1 4922777
E-mail: books@obrien.ie
Website: www.obrien.ie

ISBN: 978-1-84717-037-8

British Library Cataloguing-in-Publication Data
Nagle, Con
Selling your home : the complete Irish guide : giving your home that
winning edge
1. House selling - Ireland
I. Title
643.1'2'09415

1 2 3 4 5 6 7 8 9 10
07 08 09 10 11

Typesetting, editing, layout and design: The O'Brien Press Ltd
Printing: Cox and Wyman Ltd

CONTENTS

INTRODUCTION

There have been many 'how to sell your house' books published. They cover most of the different aspects of selling: the financial, the legal, how to negotiate, how to decorate and even how to sell without an auctioneer (normally in America). Many of these books have little if any relevance to Ireland.

Selling your home, while seldom a 'fun-filled' experience, can be a painless and profitable one if you go about the job with purpose and direction. It can be a daunting prospect. It can also be very tempting to just turn over the reins to the first estate agent you meet.

But wait. What is your goal? If you are like most people, it is to sell your home for the best price, in the shortest time and with the least hassle. Why hand over hard-earned cash to an estate agent without knowing what they will be doing to achieve these goals for you? This book sets out to help you decide whether you need an estate agent's assistance, and, if so, how you can insure that the estate agent you appoint will help you achieve your goal. Again, this is 'the best price, in the shortest time and with the least hassle'.

In my years as an estate agent, I haven't yet come across a book that explained how to choose an estate agent, and then get the most out of that agent, when you are selling your home. This amazes me, as most sellers sell through an estate agent. Yet, there are no books on how the process works. This book will explain much about what an estate agent should do for you, if you appoint one. The role of an estate agent is not simply to act as an intermediary between you and the buyer. They are acting on your behalf. It is you who are paying them.

We look also at the option of selling your home privately and at the tasks you will have to undertake should you take on the job of selling your home yourself.

I will advise you on what you or your estate agent or both of you can do to ensure that your property stands out among all the other properties currently on the market with the aim of selling your home quickly and for the most money. In the following chapters, we will look at the sales process, privately and with an estate agent, how to ensure that your property is marketed effectively, how to deal with offers and how to complete the sale. We will also consider the job of selling an apartment and liaising with property-management companies on the sale.

If you want to reap the rewards of a fast sale, you must be willing to invest your time, your imagination, your patience and even a little elbow grease. Even with an excellent estate agent, it will involve a substantial time commitment as well as a good deal of planning and research. By choosing the best option for you, be it selling privately or with an estate agent, and working to a well-thought-out plan, you are well on the way to achieving your goal.

Note: in Ireland, estate agents can be called by a number of names. 'Auctioneers', 'valuers' or 'estate agents' are the most common polite descriptions of those working in the profession. The most commonly used term is 'auctioneer', even though most property is not sold by auction. The reason for this is that estate agents must hold either an auctioneer's (or a house agent's) licence in order to trade. To obtain a licence, one currently does not need to have any past experience, nor is there any academic requirement for entry into the profession. The majority of estate agents in Ireland are academically qualified. That said, there are still many unqualified practitioners in the business.

CHAPTER 1

WHEN TO SELL
YOUR HOME

The reasons people give for selling a home are varied and complex. For some, the property is just too large, now that the children have flown the nest. Others may wish to move closer to relatives or back into a town. Many elderly people move while they are still able to make friends and fear that they might soon have reduced mobility. A growing family is another commonly cited reason.

Some reasons for selling are joyful, such as impending marriage, moving closer to home, a new job or a promotion at work. Some other good-news reasons for selling include a lotto win (yes, I've sold for somebody who won) or other financial windfall.

Other reasons are not so happy. These can include the ill health of the seller or a relative. The death of a spouse or a close relative also springs to mind. Unfortunately, for many people, they have to sell the family home due to marital difficulties, emigration, job loss or financial problems.

While it is not necessary to tell your chosen agent your reason for selling, there is no harm in confiding in them. They won't tell the world, and they are supposed to be acting for you. If you feel you can't trust them with this information, then don't appoint them to sell your home. While there might be no need, the more your agent knows about your reasons for moving, the better they can prepare a sales strategy to suit you and your property. For example, you might want to move before the children start school in September.

Regardless of your reason, there are some important factors to keep in mind when selling your house.

SELL YOUR HOUSE, NOT YOUR HOME

First, you have decided to sell a house, not your home. Your new home is where you intend to move to. You must put your personal feelings about the impending sale aside.

Of course, this is much easier said than done. Perhaps this is the first home you have ever owned or even the one where you grew up. There may be countless memories associated with the property. While it is perfectly normal to have these sentimental feelings about the place you have been living, these feelings are not going to sell your house.

In keeping with this principle, you will have to set aside your emotions and view the selling of your house objectively. You will have to appoint an estate agent and ensure that your house is presented to look and feel like a house that anybody can easily move into and create their own 'home sweet home'.

The decision to buy a home is never purely rational. Buyers buy with their hearts as well as their heads. So it is well worth your time and effort making your home warm and inviting.

WHEN TO SELL

In the past, it was generally accepted that the optimum time for selling a property was in the spring or in the autumn. The market slowed down in the summer and approaching Christmas and New Year. It was probably also impossible to find a banker, solicitor or even an auctioneer who was working in these months. It was felt that if a property was sold during the main selling months, while the market was buoyant, it was much more likely to attract the asking price.

That was in the past. People took two weeks for summer holidays, and it was their only break. Over the past number of years, the number of house sales per month has been levelling out. People are getting married, separated, moving jobs, having babies, planning for the future, etc., every month of the year. Therefore, they are moving home at all times of the year. In the modern era, when people want to buy a house, they go out and buy a house, no matter what time of the year it is.

Obviously, the longer days of the spring and summer will show off your property at its best. Also, if you have a garden, it will be easier to emphasise its features in the summer months. Having said that, some agents say that, for the past three or four years, a lot of houses sold in the first few months of the year have achieved higher prices than those selling later. This is because by agreeing to buy a property early in the year, one can have full advantage of the summer in their new home. Selling at what may be perceived as an off-peak time means that your home doesn't have to compete with as many other properties. This lack of choice for buyers can often lead to a higher price.

If you can manage viewings coming up to Christmas and the added stress of dealing with the sale of your home approaching the holidays, December could be a good time to sell. This is because the prospect of buying a new home before the end of the year is alluring to many potential buyers. It is their last chance to achieve their goal of purchasing a new home in that year.

So, the gist of the story is that, for the average home, it makes little difference what time of the year you place it on the market. There are advantages and disadvantages to all seasons. Sell whenever it is right for you and your personal circumstances.

TIME YOURSELF

One important question to ask at this point is, 'How much time do I have to sell?' The answer will dictate much of your course of action, including the price you hope to achieve as well as how aggressively you need to market your home. Timing and the current market conditions are two main factors to consider.

The quicker you need to sell your house, the less flexible you can afford to be. After all, you don't have the time to wait around for your asking price or for a more suitable time of year to place your home on the market. If you are selling your current home because you have seen a property that you want to buy, you need to move immediately. On the other hand, if you have ample time, you can sit back and wait for the perfect selling season and buyer to come along.

AVOID THE PRESSURE

It's best to put your house up for sale before you decide to buy another one. Buying and selling at the same time puts a lot of pressure on you, and you don't want to risk having to take a lower offer for your home than you expected for the sake of a quick sale. If you do decide to buy before you sell, you could put in an offer conditional on selling your current home. You cannot do this at an auction, and when demand is high, it might not work out for you on a private-treaty sale either. It will be up to the seller as to whether to accept your offer or not. In a strong market, there will be many more straightforward offers for the seller to accept. Also, while banks do offer bridging loans, these can be expensive.

The simple economic rules of supply and demand apply also to the housing market. If the market is tight and demand exceeds supply, prices go up faster, and you're in line for a good price. However, if a lot of people are selling and supply exceeds demand, prices will be under pressure, and the property will be harder to shift for the price you desire.

Of course, the market works in a cyclical fashion. Slow periods are usually immediately followed by periods of faster sales and higher prices. If the current market is especially slow and you are in no rush to sell, it is probably a good idea to ride it out and wait for an upswing.

Most of the time, we can't choose when we will place our home on the market. We need to let our own personal circumstances, be they positive or not, dictate. If you can, sell when the time suits you. If possible, do some research as to market conditions. When is the best time to sell your home? Will the time of the year affect the price for your property? Remember that there are positives to all times of the year.

CHAPTER 2

WHAT'S YOUR HOME WORTH?

In this chapter, we will discuss your property's value and how best to go about researching and ascertaining what this may be. Some, if not all, of these methods are used by Ireland's biggest and most profitable developers and builders to set prices for the thousands of homes they sell every year. We will also look at the asking price for your home and advise on how it should be set.

THE MARKET IN IRELAND

Every day bring changes to the property market. In Ireland, price increases of more than 10 per cent per year have been recorded in all but two of the past twelve years. This shows what low unemployment, a large inflow of foreign labour and relatively cheap money can do in an already house-hungry market.

What the future holds for house prices here or internationally is anybody's guess. Reasons for possible slowdowns are given, such as uncertainties in the world's economy as well as possible shocks to oil supply, interest rates, price instability, inflation, wars, etc.

Because of the above, it is extremely difficult to ascertain your property's true value in this day and age. The old adage that a property is worth what somebody is willing to pay for it is very true. The only way to be exact on its value is to sell it. But that doesn't tell you, now, what it is worth – in advance of placing it on the market. So how do you go about calculating the value of your property?

RESEARCHING THE VALUE OF YOUR PROPERTY

Just as with any product that a person may market to the general public, it is critical to know what is going on in the surrounding marketplace. Before you invite an estate agent to value your home, you need to have an idea of what your property is worth. The value of your home is usually based on some or all of the following: the price you paid for it originally, the improvements you have made and prices received by neighbours who recently sold.

It is important to have an idea of your property's value before you invite out an estate agent, for a number of reasons.

One of the tactics used by the cowboy auctioneers is to deliberately overvalue your property. Many vendors list their property with the most over-optimistic valuer who comes around to view the property. With this in mind, you can't really expect an honest valuation from some estate agent who is hoping to earn commission by listing your home with their firm. The best way to protect yourself from falling into this and other such traps is to undertake a bit of market research yourself and obtain a more precise estimate of the value of your home. While it may seem like hard work, I can guarantee that it will save you untold hassle if it helps you appoint the best agent in town. It will also help you realise a better price in less time.

The estate agent will want to get the sale of your property, and some agents will use any trick in the book to get your property on their listing and, therefore, a fee for themselves and their firm if the property is sold.

Method 1

By far the most important determinant of price is what buyers are paying right now for similar homes

in your neighbourhood. So pick up property brochures by calling into your local estate agents and register with a few as a buyer. Describe your own
property to them and get a list of relevant property
particulars. Ask them to post or e-mail you details of
any similar properties that come up for sale.

Method 2

Another way is to look through copies of the property
supplements available with all national newspapers.
If you don't have copies, you can always call to the
local library as they will normally stock back issues. A
scan of internet listings and property websites is
another similar method of finding comparable homes
and their values. You can find homes in your neighbourhood listed for sale at individual estate agents'
websites, along with the larger search engines such as
myhome.ie, daft.ie., realestate.ie and ipav.ie.

Method 3

An alternative way to get a reasonably accurate picture of your property's worth would be to take the
price you paid for it and inflate this figure by the
amount of property inflation in the intervening
period. According to the Permanent TSB House Price
Index, houses have risen in price by 270 per cent over

the past ten years, or by an average of 15 per cent per annum compounded over this time.

This is actually an easy exercise. The Central Statistics Office, Permanent TSB and others have all this information available in relatively easy-to-read formats on their websites. Check www.cso.ie or the Permanent TSB House Price Index for the average rise in prices over the past ten years – or whatever number of years it is since you bought your home.

Example 1

To work out the rough value of your house today, if it was worth €100,000 ten years ago:

€100,000 × 270 per cent

=   €270,000 = rise in price

+   <u>€100,000</u> = original price

    €370,000 = today's price

If you bought your home prior to January 2003, you would have bought it in Irish pounds. To convert the Irish pounds purchase price of your home to euro you multiply the Irish pounds purchase price of your home by 1.27, as 1 Irish pound equals 1.27 euro.

For example, IR£50,000 (× 1.27) = €63,500.

Or, IR£100,000 (× 1.27) = €127,000.

Example 2

If you purchased your house five years ago and bought it for €200,000, this is how you calculate its value today (with 15 per cent per annum growth per year over the past five years).

(€200,000) × (1.15) = €230,000

(€230,000) × (1.15) = €264,500

(€264,500) × (1.15) = €304,175

(€304,175) × (1.15) = €349,801

(€349,801) × (1.15) = €402,271 = today's price

While this method might seem crude, it can be surprisingly accurate. This calculation, or a version of it, is utilised by many estate agents, builders and developers as a check on their own calculations and prices.

Method 4

Put yourself in a buyer's shoes. Think like a buyer. What else is for sale in your neighbourhood? How does it compare with your house? How long has it been on the market? What has sold recently, and how much did the buying public value it at? What has failed to sell in the past year? What price would it take for you to look at a list and say to an estate agent, 'Take me to see that house'?

Method 5

You may also try calculating the cost per square foot of your home and comparing it to the size and prices being obtained locally. If your house has more features or other desirable qualities, you may want to set a slightly higher selling price (but not too high). Be wary of doing this, as a given street will support only a given price range. If you've invested so much that yours would be the most expensive house on the street, the buying public is not likely to reimburse you.

There are also areas and roads that command a premium and always have. There is no point in saying that your house is better decorated or bigger than the one for sale on the more desirable street if the posh street always attracts a 10- or 20-per-cent premium in prices, over and above properties on your street.

Always be sure to exercise caution and common sense, as some comparisons need to be excluded from your analysis. New homes are a prime example. Many people will pay a premium to live in a brand-new home. It is like new-car syndrome: we would all prefer to buy a new car than a second-hand one. There is also a significant stamp-duty saving when buying a new home as opposed to a second-hand one. So exclude the price of new properties from your calculations.

After you have used two or more of these methods to value your property, just get the average. It will be pretty accurate if you have done your homework. But remember the saying, 'garbage in means garbage out', so do your homework properly. Otherwise, your valuation will be off the mark and of no practical use.

SETTING THE ASKING PRICE

After you work out what your home is worth, the next thing you'll need to do is to determine your asking price. A house properly priced is half sold. But there are plenty of ways to price it improperly, especially if you have not done your homework as detailed above.

An important factor to consider when choosing the asking price is your time frame. If you are looking for a quick sale, you will probably need to consider a lower asking price. However, if your time frame is more flexible, it is possible to adjust the price you can expect to receive accordingly. A good starting point, once you determine your time frame, is to research the current market and to choose a fair price that will not only benefit you but also will attract the largest pool of buyers.

If your price is substantially higher than the going price for neighbouring homes, you will detract buyer interest and have a difficult time making a sale. On the other hand, if your asking price is too low, you do not actually risk losing money, as competition among bidders will bring your house price up to the market value if it is properly exposed and marketed.

Keep in mind that your goal is to sell your house. Of course you want to realise the most you possibly can for your property. That is why you are spending time reading this book in the first place! But by far the biggest mistake sellers tend to make is to overprice their home. Overpricing a home reduces buyer interest and makes other homes in your area look like better value than yours. It is totally counterproductive to ask for a price that is higher than comparable homes. You deter potential buyers from viewing the property, not to mind making an offer.

Overpricing is the number-one reason why some homes remain unsold for long periods. (They only sell when the market catches up to the price the owner wants or when the owner reduces the asking price.) Buyers are fully aware of prices and values of all properties within their price range and are rarely foolish when spending their hard-earned money.

By setting the asking price slightly low, you do not lose out. The market will bid up the property to its true value. However, by asking too much at the start, you scare away viewers, and you don't get any bids.

While it may seem obvious, if you have no viewers, you will have no offers and, therefore, no sale. Many people still make the mistake of setting an excessively high asking price for their home. Don't be one of them.

You should note that the market price for any property is not what you think it is worth, nor what your estate agent thinks it is worth, but, rather, what a potential buyer is willing to pay. If you set the price of your home as close as possible to the price you are willing to accept, you are likely to end up with some offers and, very probably, a sale.

Finally, set the price at just under a round number: for example, €369,000 instead of €370,000. It's the old supermarket trick, but it works. The figure €369,000 sounds like a lot less than €370,000, just as €9.99 is psychologically less than €10. All multinational retailers, from our own Dunnes Stores and Tesco, to Wal-Mart, Sony and Dell all do it. They sell many billions of euro worth of products every year, so learn from them and price your property accordingly.

CHAPTER 3

CHOOSING
AN ESTATE AGENT

Do you really need an auctioneer to help you sell your home? Legally speaking, you don't, but then again you don't need to go to a dentist if you want a tooth taken out. You could take it out yourself. But it's probably not a good idea. The same argument could be made about whether you need an estate agent.

People can sell their own properties themselves, but the overwhelming majority believe that they are better served by an experienced and qualified professional. It is really only in the USA that there is much of an appetite for sellers to attempt to sell their own property. Much of this is due to the fact that estate agents (or realtors, as they are called there) charge fees of between 6 and 8 per cent of the property's value.

Here in Ireland the auctioneer's fees are at about one quarter of this rate. While there are no official government figures available, a recent survey (2007) by the Confederation of European Estate Agents (CEI) found that 95 per cent of all property sold in Ireland is with the assistance of a professional (see the graph on p. 46). Some property commentators believe that if you exclude property transferred between relatives and therefore not available to the general market, this figure would be closer to 99 per cent.

A good auctioneer will undoubtedly help you real-ise the best possible price and conditions for the sale of your home. They will also have a significant impact on whether the sale of your home progresses in a timely and orderly fashion.

You should use an estate agent if you believe that they will achieve a better price for your property, faster than you could yourself and with less hassle than if you attempt to sell it yourself. A qualified auc-tioneer has the knowledge and experience plus the back-up of an 'in-place' organisation that can effec-tively advertise and promote your home to potential buyers. They should have a list of customers who are actively looking for a property in your locality. Your agent will also be able to accurately determine the market value and the best selling price of your home.

This should ensure confidence that the price you are accepting is indeed the true market value and that you are not losing out by accepting any offer that they recommend.

THE GOOD, THE BAD AND THE UGLY

One cannot stress too strongly that all estate agents are not the same. Your choice of agent is of great importance. It can make the difference between a fast and fairly painless process and one that drags on for an eternity, with nothing to show at the end (except a large advertising and outlay bill owed to the auction-eering firm).

In Ireland at the moment, there is an extremely large pool of auctioneers to choose from. Some are experienced professionals while others are, and there is no other way to put it, pure chancers. Individuals who were selling insurance, or bankers, failed engineers, politicians, former pub-owners and undertakers have all taken out auctioneer's licences in the past few years. Many have nothing to offer but their ability to talk.

To the casual observer, all auctioneers are the same. But they most certainly are not (take my word, and don't find out through a painful experience). The dif-ference in the service provided by a dedicated and professional estate agent over their incompetent

competitor can be like comparing chalk and cheese.
Don't be afraid to ask the agent some questions:

- How long have they been auctioneering?
- How large is their firm?
- How many full-time and qualified estate agents
  will be responsible for selling your property?
- Why do they feel that their firm is the right one to
  handle the sale of your property?
- Do they have a database of clients looking for
  property?
- Do they have the required bonds and insurance?

There is a major difference between purchasing a
service, such as an auctioneer's service, and a commodity. When you buy a commodity – a fridge or a
car, for example – you normally get a guarantee. You
get what you pay for. Many of us are willing to pay
more for a superior product. For example, if all cars
were of the same quality, nobody would be paying
extra for a Lexus, Mercedes or BMW. We'd all be driving cars that cost the same.

This is not true for services, be they financial (as in
banking or insurance), accountancy, legal or estate-
agency. The best agent in your locality will probably
be able to obtain thousands of euro more for your
property than his or her least effective competitor.
With property prices being what they are, and every

euro important, it pays to choose the right agent for the job. If you are discerning enough to pay extra for a quality car, stereo, wide-screen television or family holiday, why not pay for the best estate agent? The difference in fees between a good and a bad agent will be negligible, whereas the difference in price achieved may be measured in thousands or even tens of thousands of euro.

The question then is how to choose the best agent to market and sell your home. To choose the best estate agent for your property, personal recommendations are invaluable. Ask your family, friends, boss or work acquaintances to see if they received a good service from any agents. Be sure to ask if they were happy with the service, as I once came across a seller who asked a relative if they knew any auctioneers. They gave her a name, and she hired that person's firm to sell her home. Six months later she met the relative again and complained that the agent was hopeless. But, as the relative then pointed out, she had only asked if he knew any agents – not if he could recommend one.

The factors that differentiate an excellent agent and firm from an average or below-average one can be viewed under a large variety of headings. The ones that I have chosen are mainly related to the marketing and advertising of homes. They are, 'For Sale' sign presence, office location, quality of website, qualifications and professionalism and the standard of the firm's property brochures. The estate agent for you is the one who will market your home best and, therefore, give you the best chance of an excellent price, in a speedy manner.

Look for 'For Sale' signs

Be sure to look around for 'For Sale' and 'Sold' signs in your locality to see who's busy and what companies are selling most in your area. Agents' signs are one of the most important indicators as to which agents are active and successful. The first step is to take note of all the auctioneering firms with signs up in your area. People in your neighbourhood have chosen these agents as the best estate agent to sell for them. Pay particular attention to 'Sale Agreed' and 'Sold' signs, as these are what you want outside your house in a few weeks' time. The agent who has sold most in your locality could be the one who will best serve you. At the very least they deserve to be on any shortlist of agents you decide to meet.

Office location

Most potential purchasers call in to the main agents in any particular town in which they have an interest in purchasing. Therefore, it is vital to list your property with an agent who has a presence in the locality. Check that the office is well kept and that the reception staff are courteous, competent and willing to help.

Website

Has your chosen estate agent their own dedicated website? If they have not invested in their own website, disregard them from the reckoning. By only directing interested parties for your home to a generic site, such as myhome.ie or daft.ie, they are forcing your property to compete with numerous other properties. They are not capturing enquiries for your specific property. Their website should be easy to navigate, and properties should be professionally displayed. It should also be updated regularly and well publicised.

Qualifications

Ensure your agent is a member of either the IAVI or the IPAV. Are all of the firm's sales staff who will be dealing with and showing your property members of the IPAV or the IAVI? If they are, this ensures that they are trained professionals and abide by the rules and regulations of their institute. Breaches of these rules lead to investigations and sanctions, as both bodies have strong disciplinary procedures.

It takes time and dedication to obtain these qualifications. If your estate agent or the firm's staff have not invested in their education, don't risk the sale of your property to them.

Standard of property brochure

It is vital, on a number of counts, to have a professional information sheet or brochure when selling your home. Ensure that features such as square footage/metreage, number of bedrooms and bathrooms, etc., are included on the brochure. Sometimes a brochure must sell a neighbourhood as well as a house. If so, desirable local amenities such as schools, shops, playgrounds and local transport should be included. Compare the property brochures of a number of the auctioneers you are thinking of appointing.

Auctioneer's licence

Ensure that your chosen estate agent is licensed. To act in the selling of property, an auctioneer must be licensed by the district court and hold a valid auctioneer's licence. If you have never heard of the firm before, ask to see a copy of their licence. By law, it must be displayed in a prominent position within their office.

Insurance

Have they got professional indemnity insurance? This is vital so that they can cover the cost of any claims for negligence that you or other disgruntled vendors may bring against them. Again, if they have been around for a long period of time, it is safe to assume that this is in place – but ask if you have any doubts.

A number of auctioneers go bust practically every year, and clients have lost out financially. So use a reputable, licensed and insured agent.

NATIONAL OR 'BRANDED FIRM' VERSUS STRONG LOCAL FIRM

Should you place your property with a large auctioneering firm, a national 'brand name' or a strong more local operator? This is a question I am often asked. While there is no right or wrong answer, why not ask yourself which firm wants your business more or who will get you the most for your home?

Many people are seduced by the lure of the big name, but size can lead to inefficiencies. This is especially the case in the services industry, such as in auctioneering services. The management structure of large operators is complicated. There is a long chain of command, and decision-making becomes less responsive to the market. It is very difficult for decision-makers in large firms to keep in touch with the grass roots as customer contact is remote or non-existent. On the other hand, the small to medium-sized auctioneering firm can operate from a number of local offices. Communication lines are short. Supervision is in the hands of the owner or manager, and decisions are made on the spot. The smaller estate-agency firms are locally based and develop close contact with their customers. They know what is happening in the market in which you are selling. If they have a number of local offices, the owner or a manager has personal responsibility for running the firm.

But beware: some single-office firms are small because they are new. (Do you want them to be learning at the expense of thousands of euro lost on your sale?) Sometimes they are small because they are just bad at their job. There is no barrier to entry in the auctioneering business. The capital required to start up is small, and licences are very easy to get.

Be sure to avoid the 'one-man band' auctioneer who operates without the necessary staff to do the job. I know of more than one auctioneering practice that doesn't show properties for a number of weeks over the summer while the owner goes on holidays.

THE BEAUTY PARADE

Having reviewed all the possible contenders for your business, it is now time to become serious about appointing an estate agent. Compile a shortlist of between two and four auctioneering firms that you are reasonably comfortable with from preliminary analysis. Normally any more than this is a waste of your time and theirs.

Most of the time, the choice of firm comes down to a compromise. The 'all-singing, all-dancing' salesperson in one office may fail to follow up an enquiry, while the shabbily dressed agent in a poorly presented office might be the winner in other categories. Sometimes, you have a choice of only one. If so, I hope that's because they win hands down in all your chosen categories, rather than because they are the only agent in town.

The next step is to arrange a valuation appointment or 'beauty parade' of the chosen few. This is a reasonably big responsibility, and if you can, have a partner, family member or trusted friend present also. It's an onerous responsibility, so two heads are better than one. Don't be afraid to tell the invited auctioneers that you are inviting a few agents. This will keep them on their toes – but don't tell them exactly who else is coming.

If you are arranging all the appointments for the one day, it is advisable to give about an hour and a half to each one. You don't want competing agents meeting at the door – it is embarrassing for all concerned. Allowing sufficient time gives the agent a chance to explain their service fully. It is strongly preferable that all valuation appointments be undertaken before darkness falls as it is unfair to expect any estate agent to accurately value your property after dark.

Finally, pick a time for the valuation that suits you. An old trick used by estate agents is to pretend they are busy in order to impress potential clients. They will probably be able to alter or move another appointment to get a chance of your listing, if you insist.

Interview prospective estate agents for your business with care. Your chances of selling quickly and with the least hassle, which is what this book is all about, are improved considerably by appointing the right experienced and professional estate agent. Sellers tell me horror stories from when they were selling their home. Most of these people chose their auctioneer badly. Many had picked the cheapest firm in the locality, or the large 'national' franchise, and they had a horrible time of it. But don't tar all auctioneers with the same brush. Like all professions, there are 'the good, the bad and the truly ugly'. The choice is yours.

REAP THE BENEFITS

A good reputable firm of auctioneers will not only help you determine how much your home is worth, They will also price the property according to their proven sales strategy, market it professionally and competently and negotiate with interested parties. More importantly, they will help you judge whether prospective buyers have the finance to purchase your home or are just wasting your time. They will also assist and coordinate many of the legal and financial transactions involved in closing the sale.

The most effective estate agent, from your point of view, is one who knows about the neighbourhood. They can answer questions that are important to potential buyers of your home, about schools, places of worship, medical facilities and other services available in the community.

The right auctioneer will actively work to find buyers for your house. They will have a well-thought-out plan for marketing your house to the right target audience. Look for the company with enthusiasm and a positive attitude, not the fast talk. Do not automatically hire the professional who promises that he or she can sell your house at the highest price. Look instead for the estate agent that provides the most realistic and optimistic assessment of the marketability of your home, based on current home-sales data.

A good estate agent, and their firm, will attract many more potential purchasers for your property than an inexperienced rookie or a lazy estate agent. The decision is yours.

AGENCY

There are different types of agency you can grant for the sale of your property. These are sole agency, joint agency and open agency.

Sole agency means that you have given a single auctioneering firm the rights to sell your property, to the exclusion of other firms, during the lifetime of the agency. Sole agency is the predominant type of agency given. Should the sole agent introduce a buyer, there is no dispute as to which agent is due the fee. Sole agency is the most common type of agency and is used in more than 95 per cent of cases.

A **joint agency** is where two or more estate agents are appointed to act together in the marketing and sale of your property. They are working as a team, and they will all receive a share of the agreed fee in the event of the introduction of a ready, willing and able buyer at a price acceptable to you. Naturally, with two agents involved, fees are higher than in the case of a sole agency.

Open agency is where the property is placed on a number of estate agents' books, on a competitive, winner-takes-all basis. With open agencies, astute buyers can, and will, approach every agent that has the property for sale. The potential buyer will naturally select the estate agent that promises to sell the property to them at the lowest price. When you think about that, you know it cannot be in your interest to go down the open-agency route.

Sole agents or joint agents are also far more certain to receive a fee than a firm working on an open-agency basis. This naturally concentrates the firm's efforts on your behalf, and, in most cases, you get a higher price for your property.

Selling rights

When you grant a sole, joint or open agency, you usually retain the right to sell the property yourself. Before you think this is an easy opt-out, bear in mind that this can only be to someone introduced to you without any input whatsoever from the agent. Even a buyer seeing the agent's 'For Sale' sign on the property and knocking on your door means that the agent was instrumental in introducing the buyer to you (via their sign) and is entitled to their fees. The courts have upheld this principle.

Estate-agency contracts

Read the estate agent's terms of business or contract, including any small print, carefully, as you may find yourself signed up and legally bound for a long period of time. If this is the case, in the event of poor service, you will not be able to go elsewhere to get your property sold, unless, of course, you are prepared to fork out two fees. If you're not (and who is?), insist on an agreement for a reasonable time period only.

AUCTIONEER'S FEES

You should not do business with any agent unless you have agreed a fee in advance. Your agent will confirm this to you in writing before commencing work on your behalf. Ensure that you receive a professional service from the start.

One dishonest tactic to watch out for is if the agent says they won't charge VAT on their fees. (Auctioneer's fees are normally quoted as a set percentage plus VAT, that is, for example, 1.5 per cent plus VAT at 21 per cent). This VAT discount, as you can imagine, sounds very attractive to the gullible seller. Not charging the VAT amounts to a reduction of 21 per cent in the professional fees you, the seller, pay. There is only one problem. It is illegal and dishonest, and when the auctioneer double-crosses you, as they will, and takes the auctioneer's fees plus 21 per cent VAT out of the booking deposit paid on your property, you have no recourse. You cannot sue them as, your solicitor will inform you, you cannot sue for enforcement of an illegal agreement.

When is the auctioneer's fee earned?

An estate agent or auctioneer is normally deemed to have earned the agreed (legal) fee once they introduce a ready, willing and able buyer at a price acceptable to you. The fee is earned and becomes payable in such circumstances, even if you withdraw from the sale for any reason.

Where a deposit is taken from a ready, willing and able buyer and you, as vendor, refuse to instruct your solicitor to send out the contract, or you refuse to go through with the sale, the deposit is fully refundable on demand to the would-be buyer. The agent has the right to sue you for fees on the basis that the professional task for which you agreed to pay has been performed, even if you decide not to benefit from it by refusing to proceed with the sale.

In the vast majority of sales that proceed to completion, the agent will usually account for any part of the deposit held by him on the closing of the sale, after deducting agreed fees and outlay due. Where the agent holds no deposit, it would be normal for you to instruct your solicitor to discharge the agent's agreed fees and outlay on the closing of the sale from the sale's proceeds.

Liability for two fees

There are circumstances where you can become liable to pay two different estate agents a fee for selling your property. If you switch agents, it may emerge that the eventual buyer has already been in contact with the original agent about your property and may even have made an offer to buy it. Should that buyer purchase through another agent, the first agent might also have a legitimate claim to have their fee paid by you, depending on the terms of the agency agreement you had with them.

OUTLAY

The outlay, including advertising spend incurred by your estate agent, is usually payable by you, regardless of whether a sale occurs. It is an extremely foolish agent who doesn't recoup outlay expenditure, such as that on advertising, signs or other such costs from clients.

A NOTE ON AGENT FEES

Auctioneer's fees in Ireland are the cheapest in western Europe, if not the world (see the graph overleaf; see also p. 28). Irish estate agents will charge you somewhere between 1 and 3 per cent of the sale price (plus VAT at 21 per cent) depending on the price of your property or where in the country you live. For some higher priced or prestigious homes, mainly in the Dublin market, some agents will do the job for an even smaller fee. This is especially so when the market is strong and when they are sure that the property will sell without much difficulty.

While it is possible to negotiate a discount with some agents, be careful; ask yourself why they are willing to give you a discount. Are they cheap because it is the only way they can get the sale of property? Will they give in as easily when it comes to negotiating a sales price on your home? There is a saying in the profession that goes, 'if somebody cannot negotiate a good fee for themselves, how can they negotiate a good price for your property?' With experience, and often costly experience, many people have found this statement to be very true. At the end of the day, auctioneer's fees will not make or break you.

Let me tell you a true story about a lady who refused to pay any fees and how she got on. Let's call her Mrs

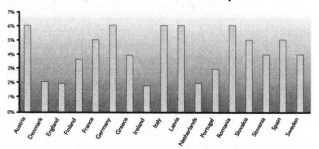

Comparative analysis of agents' commission rates across Europe

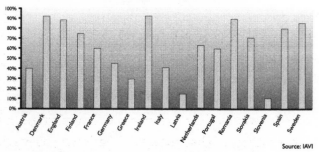

Agents' percentage market share of property transactions in European states

Source: IAVI

Murphy. It's not her name, but it's a good Cork name, and it is the only part of the story I have changed.

I rang Mrs Murphy after seeing a classified advert she had placed in the newspaper advertising her home for sale. She informed me immediately that she didn't need an auctioneer, as we were too expensive and she could sell her house herself. That was fine with me. We chatted, and she told me her asking price – which seemed extremely low. I asked her if she minded if I gave her a call in three weeks' time (as this is about the time frame for many people to decide that selling their home themselves is not for them).

After three weeks had elapsed, I duly gave Mrs Murphy a call. She was delighted. She had remembered my call from earlier, and she told me that she had an offer of her asking price on the first day of viewing, to a nice man who was extremely anxious to move in. Her solicitor had issued contracts, and the purchaser has signed and returned them immediately. She was delighted she had saved the auctioneer's fees. The house price was €125,000, so she saved between €2,000 and €3,000 in fees. The problem was that no sooner had the sale closed than there was a 'For Sale' sign in the garden of the house. The 'nice man who wanted to move in immediately' knew that he was getting an absolute steal. That's why he was in a hurry with the contracts. He sold the property within two months of purchasing it, for in excess of €200,000 – a €75,000 profit. Mrs Murphy saved herself auctioneer's fees but lost out on €75,000. I know this story to be true, as I spoke with Mrs Murphy prior to her selling her home, and, to cap it all, my firm (by coincidence) was appointed to sell for Mrs Murphy's nice man. He had no trouble in paying auctioneer's fees.

CHAPTER 4

SELLING WITHOUT AN ESTATE AGENT

In some countries, the do-it-yourself approach to selling one's own home is well established. In Ireland this is not yet the case, although in the past few years there have been a number of companies and websites set up to assist vendors to sell their own homes. Just type the letters 'FSBO', which stands for 'for sale by owner', into any internet search engine, and you will get a selection of Irish responses, along with thousands of foreign ones.

The FSBO industry, especially in America, believes that this is a more cost-efficient way to buy and sell property. The argument goes that home-buyers and -sellers are much smarter than ever before and that by merging the technology of the Internet together with the knowledge and support of a dedicated FSBO website, house-owners will achieve the best possible results with the least amount of time and effort.

The number of independent property sales is starting to rise as is the number of property websites assisting all sellers, auctioneers and private sellers. Apartments and properties in housing estates are easier to sell online than detached homes, especially if you live in a popular area where you can be sure of strong demand.

You do not necessarily need to use an auctioneer when it comes to selling your home, and there is no legal reason why a homeowner cannot sell their property themselves. The Irish house-owning public is extremely well educated, and many excel in sales roles of many kinds. People now have the necessary confidence in their abilities, and many feel that they could make as good a job of selling their home as an auctioneer. In truth, they probably could – if they are willing to put in the time and effort. The question is, then, whether they are indeed able to give the task the time and effort it requires. Nothing in this world is as easy as we first think. Many professionals of all kinds can make their jobs look easy. We often only see the final product and not all the work that goes on behind the scenes.

First, begin by making an informed decision on whether to sell privately as opposed to using an estate agent. Going down the do-it-yourself route is a big decision to take. Be sure to take it for the right reasons. Let's examine why you are considering selling by yourself. The main arguments for selling one's home by utilising the services of one of these websites can be summarised below. I will let you decide on their relative merits.

SAVING MONEY ON FEES

Obviously, saving money is one of the main motivations for selling your home yourself. House prices have climbed steadily over time; therefore, by selling their home privately, homeowners can potentially save thousands of euros. By not paying auctioneers fees of between 1 and 2 per cent (plus 21 per cent VAT), substantial savings can be made. For example, if you sell your home for €250,000, typical auctioneer's fees, including VAT, would amount to between €3,000 and €6,000. Savings are even higher the more valuable your property is. At a price of €350,000, the figure is between €4,200 and €8,500. This is the amount you can save by selling your home privately, always assuming you get as much for it as an auctioneer would have done. There is no point in putting in a large effort to save money on fees if you are only shaving a similar amount off your selling price. Anyone contemplating going down the private-sale route should consider whether there will be any financial savings at the end of the day.

SELL YOUR HOME FASTER

Another often-quoted reason for selling privately is that without the auctioneer's fees you can sell your home faster. Because you are not paying selling fees, you can afford to price your home more aggressively. The lower the price, the more likely it will sell fast. If the amount that you have reduced the price by is less than the amount the agent's fees would have been, you might walk away with possibly thousands in savings, and you will just be doing it faster.

Some feel that if you list your home with an estate agent, you'll probably inflate the asking price to cover the cost of their fees. Later, you risk coming to the painful realisation that no one is going to buy your home at that price, and you'll end up reducing the price (or accepting an offer) equal to the original amount you would have asked if selling privately. In order to sell faster, you may reduce your price by the amount of fees you are saving, and, therefore, you do not end up making any real saving.

In countries with much higher estate-agent fees, these two reasons might make very good sense. I'm not sure that a 1 or 2 per cent discount to a home makes any perceptible difference in its selling time.

Most people selling property in Ireland and Great Britain currently use an estate agent. There is a strong correlation between countries with high estate-agent fees and the number of property transactions completed without agents. For example, in Ireland, England and Denmark, where fees are less than 2 per cent of the property value, about 90 per cent of property transactions are undertaken with the assistance of agents. (See the graph on p. 46.) At the other end of the scale, in countries such as Germany, Austria, Italy and Latvia, fees are high, and estate agents are involved in only about half of all property transactions.

IT'S SO EASY

'Despite what an auctioneer may say, selling a house is not rocket science. If you can sell your own car, you can sell your own home . . . it's that simple' says one of the FSBO websites. But wait a minute. Many cars at the side of the road never get sold at the original asking price. How many friends of yours have decided that they can get far more for their car than the garage was offering in a trade-in scenario? Months later, the car might still be outside their front door, sometimes a year older and much less valuable. So let's knock that old chestnut on the head; it is not easy selling your home for a good price – but it can be done. This book will help you to do so.

Another often-quoted reason for selling privately is 'Less hassle and frustration'. When selling privately, you don't have to leave the house because an agent wants to show it or clean it every morning before leaving 'just in case'. You know when people are coming and can prepare accordingly. And when a buyer makes an offer, there's not all that frustrating back-and-forth telephone tag between agents to reach an agreement. It can be done in minutes and end with a friendly handshake and smile between owner and buyer.

Furthermore, because you meet the prospective buyers, you have a much better idea how interested people are, what they like about the home, how serious they are about buying and what their time frame and situation is. The direct feedback is easier to live with than wondering how things are going or wondering why no one has made an offer yet.

You also know your home best. The schools, the neighbourhood – you know what is special about the area, as well as other details about the property. A well-maintained, fairly priced home virtually sells itself. So the seller's role is simply to provide additional information. Some estate agents use poorly qualified staff and poor negotiators to show properties. Homeowners could certainly do as good a job as some of those agents when showing and selling their own property.

Nobody is going to tell you what to do. You can advertise where and how you want to, schedule showings when it's convenient for you, talk directly with prospective buyers yourself, even take your house off the market for a while if you can't find the right house to move to. Furthermore, you aren't obliged to commit to staying with an estate agent for a three-, six- or twelve-month contract . . . you make your own rules.

THE GAME PLAN

So, you have made your decision and are selling privately. What is your game plan? A homeowner's success in selling by themselves depends on many factors such as asking price (in relation to the house's true market value), condition, location, competition, time of year, exposure to the market, buyers' motivation, your motivation, interest rates, the economy – along with your patience, willingness and ability to negotiate – and, sometimes, to compromise.

SETTING YOUR PRICE

First of all, you need to price your home correctly. In this regard, life is no different than if you are selling through an estate agent. Your first step is to research the asking prices of similar properties currently for sale in your area. Decide if any improvements, cosmetic or otherwise, will raise the value of your home or even if they will just make it easier to sell. (See Chapter 2 for more information on setting your asking price.)

Once you have agreed a sale with a buyer, all the legal work is dealt with by your solicitor and the buyer's solicitor. However, some sales do crumble because the potential buyer doesn't have the necessary mortgage approval, so to minimise the risk of this, ask for a deposit, made payable to your solicitor. To make sure they are serious, do what the agents do, which is to go through the questioning drill: Are they a first-time buyer? Are they selling another house? Is it sold yet? Are the contracts signed? Do they have mortgage approval in place already? And is it enough to enable them to buy your home?

The private sale of one's principal asset could turn out to be 'penny-wise but pound-foolish'. An experienced and competent auctioneer should be able to squeeze the best price out of potential buyers, using experience and various pressure tactics to convince the buyer to increase their bids beyond their original intentions. Moving home can be one of the most stressful experiences in your lifetime, so why not get an agent to do the work for you? You have to decide yourself whether selling privately is for you, based on your experiences, your personality, your skill set and your time commitments.

CHAPTER 5

MARKETING YOUR HOME

Your second-hand home has to compete with new homes, and so your marketing has to compete with new homes also. We are all familiar with going to see a show house at a new development. There are flags flying, the lawn is perfectly cut, and everything is presented immaculately. The marketing equivalents of 'bells and whistles' are everywhere. Furthermore, everybody likes something that's new – even the words 'second-hand home' don't conjure up excitement. This is what you have to compete with when selling your home.

Auctioneers often say that only three things matter when valuing a property. These are location, location and location. When marketing your home, there are, again, only three things that matter: exposure, exposure and exposure. That's how you sell your home faster and for more money.

Luring prospective buyers to your home does not have to be a challenging task. There are always going to be people looking to move. It is your estate agent's job to spread the word that you have a fabulous home on the market and to differentiate your home from the others for sale in your area. Above all, their task is to advertise your home as quickly and as cost-efficiently as possible.

If you are selling with an estate agent, they will be marketing your home through their channels. These channels include people who have previously viewed similar homes with them, people who sold with them, people who have enquired about property with them and people who have left their names on their database. If selling privately, that marketing job is up to you.

If marketed correctly, your property should sell at its best price in the least time possible. The marketing platform should include an excellently presented property brochure, photographs, a 'For Sale' sign and an internet listing, along with relevant press advertising. This will then ensure that you achieve the highest price possible for your property.

PROPERTY BROCHURE

It is vital, on a number of counts, to have a professional information sheet or brochure for your home.

Ensure that features such as square footage/metreage, number of bedrooms and bathrooms, etc., are included. A brochure must sell your neighbourhood as well as your house: desirable local amenities such as schools, shops, playgrounds and local transport should be included, where relevant.

You are possibly your home's best salesperson, so assist your auctioneer with the brochure. Provide them with information about your property and what attracted you to it in the first place. Check the proof of the brochure carefully when they send it to you for approval. It is also to everybody's advantage to clarify the fixtures, fittings and contents which are to be included, excluded or optional in the sale.

The purpose of a brochure is to get somebody to *view* the property, not to sell it. Interested parties will still need to view the property.

Your approved brochure should be circulated around your estate agent's internal and external networks. It should also be sent to their enquiry database of people registered with them as looking for a property like yours. (You did check that they had one, didn't you?)

If you are selling your home yourself, prepare a professional-looking brochure to give to anybody who wishes to view your home and use it as part of the marketing. It is worth spending time on this task, as your brochure can also provide the basis of your web advertisement. Auctioneers have invested a lot of time and money designing property brochures. While there are subtle changes of emphasis between different firms, many property brochures and particulars are relatively similar. So, don't reinvent the wheel, study the brochures of the firms which you consider best and decide which features to adopt.

Most property brochures include a photograph of the front of the house on the front page. Ensure that your product, in this case your home, looks its best before taking this and any other photographs you wish to include. See opposite for advice on preparing your home for the photographs.

Include dimensions and descriptions of all rooms. While it might not be practical to include a photograph of all rooms on printed brochures, consider posting the photographs on the web version. Information on any appliances included in the sale along with information on local amenities and special features should also be included.

It goes without saying that your contact telephone number(s) and website details should also be given, as well as what times suit you best to take enquiries.

It might also be a good idea to include a disclaimer

on any brochures, web and hard copy. Legally, property sales are ruled by the phrase *Caveat emptor*, buyer beware, and it is up to the buyer to check out all property details; however, you do not want to be taken to court because of some mistake on your brochure, so be sure to check that all the details are accurate.

PHOTOGRAPHS

If you want to attract a buyer, start by catching their eye. Before a buyer ever makes it to your front door, the introduction they may have had to your home might be the pictures included in the advertising – either your or your estate agent's website or brochure or in the estate agent's office window.

It pays to ensure that everyone uses photographs that show your home in its best light. You spend hundreds of euro to get quality portraits of your family, so don't skimp when it comes to selling your home. Why not get a professional photographer to provide internal and external photographs? Alternatively, if you have good photos of your property, ask your estate agent to use them. They will be only too delighted.

When taking a photo of your home, be sure that the front garden and driveway are uncluttered and that your house is as picture-perfect as can be. A little effort goes a long way. Stand in front of your home and take a visual assessment. How do the blinds in the bedroom window look? Does the house look more welcoming with the curtains in the living room drawn or open? Normally, open curtains are best. Cut the grass and trim any shrubs or trees. Remove toys, sports equipment, pets and their accessories from the garden. Put the bin into the garage and close any doors and gates. Park your car out of view and ensure that it's a sunny day before you pull out the camera. The best time of day to photograph your home will depend upon which direction it faces. You'll want the sun behind you, shining on the front of your home and making *it* shine.

Your estate agent may decide to include interior photos. If this is the case, don't include photos of every room: choose the rooms which are special or unique. (Perhaps your kitchen has a terrific breakfast counter.) People always want to see the master bedroom and the family room. Make sure that any room you choose to photograph is clean, tidy and well lit. Take photos from several angles and select the ones that best showcase the features or dimensions of the room.

A word of caution: while they say 'a picture is worth a thousand words', and in this case it may be worth thousands of euro, many estate agents do not recommend internal photographs. There are a number of reasons for this. Good internal shots require a wide-angle lens, suitable lighting and correct focus. Second, it is many agents' opinion that if you show people too much of the property, either on the Internet or in a brochure format, they may well decide not to view on the basis of a badly taken photo and not on the basis of the suitability of the house for their needs.

When selling your home, a photograph's purpose is not to sell the house but to sell the appointment from which the house has a chance of being sold. One extra bid can be worth thousands of euro. The whole purpose of including photos is to catch a buyer's eye and to make them want to view the property.

'FOR SALE' SIGNS

Many people who are looking for a new home will first decide on a list of areas in which they'd like to live and then drive around those areas looking for available properties. Make sure your sign can be easily seen from a distance (after all, you want those drivers to be able to write down the phone number from their car).

For more than 50 per cent of purchasers, the old-fashioned 'For Sale' sign, either directly or indirectly, was the first point of contact. Therefore, 'For Sale' signs are still one of the most important marketing tools for home-sellers. They attract attention to your home. They are also one of the easiest things to do to market your property. A 'For Sale' sign in front of your home will let everyone in the area know that you are selling. When selling privately, your motto should be to shout the fact that your home is for sale from the highest rooftops. Your sign will do this effectively.

Estate agents' signboards are distinctive and are well known in the locality they serve, and they advertise and draw attention to your property as well as to the estate agent very effectively. A large proportion of calls to your estate agent are due to their signs. It's amazing how many callers to our offices start with, 'I was driving past and I saw one of your signs'. Obviously, a house on a busy street will attract more attention than a house on a cul-de-sac. Even so, a sign is a strong and effective source of word-of-mouth referrals from your neighbours and passers-by.

Your estate agents will organise and erect a suitable signboard at your property. Some estate agents charge extra for this service, and some have it included in their percentage fee. Be sure to ask in advance.

If your house is on a quiet street with little passing traffic, your auctioneer may place a small directional sign leading in from the main street. Be guided by your estate agent on the use of these signs, as in some parts of the country they are not allowed.

A final note on auctioneer's signs. It amazes me how so many estate agents use old and tattered signs or signs with broken or poorly painted poles. A poorly hung sign will detract from the otherwise attractive appearance of your home. Even worse, a bad sign could turn off potential buyers by causing them to wonder what else you have tried to cut corners on.

A further significant advantage is that a well-placed sign assists potential viewers to find your property and to be on time for their appointment. How often have you driven around an area looking for a house number, especially on a wet day, when it's very hard to see a house number or a house name. Ensure that viewers are not frustrated before they get to view your home by making it easy for them to find your house. Their mood will be better and your chances of selling to them are improved.

It is easy enough to design your own 'For Sale' board. Any good sign-maker should be able to do it for you. Make sure that it is double-sided, and consider getting a spare one when you are having it made. The wind might knock one down or damage it, especially in wintertime.

Your sign should be clearly visible from a passing car. The most standard type of auctioneer's 'For Sale' board measures two feet by either two feet or two feet and six inches. It should be placed on a secure pole at a height that will attract passing motorists but will not knock against the heads of passing cyclists or pedestrians. If secured to a boundary, ensure that the board is not sticking out into the path or road. Ensure that the sign-maker leaves enough room on the sign for the pole. There should be a three-inch strip set aside for this.

What information should be included on your 'For Sale' sign? Apart from the words 'For Sale', it is a good idea to tell potential viewers that you are selling privately, so you will want to include the words, 'By Owner', 'Privately', 'Private Sale', 'Owner Selling' or some such words. The choice is entirely up to you. Be sure also to include a telephone number. Consider buying a specific mobile phone for this. That way, if you are out, or if there are two or more parties selling the property, whoever has the phone is on duty to take the calls. Finally, be sure to also include the web address for the property so that people can access all the relevant information.

INTERNET ADVERTISING

The Internet is emerging as another medium for selling real estate. Exposure is extremely high among the twenty-five- to forty-year-old bracket, the important home-buying ages. Many home-buyers start their search online (and this number continues to grow), though not as many as look for the old-fashioned 'For Sale' signs. The Internet is a fast and cost-effective way to reach millions of buyers, and it's for these reasons that your home should be online. It is to your advantage to advertise online as the Internet is an efficient way to bring your property to the attention of millions of people. For a nominal fee you can advertise online, including colour photos and even floor plans on some websites. This cost-effective and comprehensive mode of advertising is an excellent option for selling your home. Don't forget that the principles that relate to property brochures still apply: the aim of a web listing and all internet marketing you undertake is to set up an appointment to view your property.

To maximise the chance of a speedy, satisfactory sale, you should list your property on a website that will give you access to buyers in Ireland and overseas who would not normally check out your estate agent's window or website.

Some of the most popular websites are as follows:
- www.daft.ie
- ww.ipav.ie
- www.myhome.ie
- www.propertynews.com
- www.realestate.ie.

Alternatively, just type FSBO (for sale by owner) into a search engine to locate relevant websites.

PRESS ADVERTISING

Your estate agent should submit a press release to the property editors in relevant newspapers in an attempt to get you some free editorial coverage throughout the marketing campaign for your property. Bear in mind that actual publication is at the discretion of the individual property editors, and no estate agent can guarantee that the content will be as you might wish.

More conventional newspaper advertising guarantees maximum exposure to buyers at a reasonable cost. As I have mentioned, exposing your property to potential purchasers is the single most important investment in achieving the highest price possible. Newspaper advertising is still an important element in this. Personally, I would never sell a property that I owned without advertising it in the property section of the local and national newspapers. Press advertising should include at least one photographic advert in the property supplement of the chosen paper, along with a selection of classified adverts. Your adverts should provide the critical points which buyers are looking for, such as location, house type and the number of bedrooms.

A few hundred euro or even a few thousand euro spent on newspaper advertising, depending on the value of your property, is money well spent when selling your home. Just look at the size and regularity of builder's adverts for their new developments. They know the power of press advertising and use it accordingly.

A good advert grabs the reader's attention with a catchy headline. Think back to what motivated you to buy your home in the first place and put it in a headline. For example:

> **Spacious living:** 3-bedroom home, on cul-de-sac near schools and shopping. € price. Nothing like it at this price! Tel: 01-2345678 at any time.
> www.youraddresshere.ie

'A spacious home!', 'a quiet retreat!', 'private', 'convenient location!', 'spectacular views' are all examples of catchy headlines. You can probably think of a better one for your home, and the following list of headlines and ideas that sell may also be of help.

Setting

Tucked away
South-facing
Relaxing environment
Charming country cottage
Stunning woodland setting
Enviably located
Leafy suburb
Private setting
Superbly located
Prestigious location
Tranquil setting
Family friendly location
High level of privacy
Overlooking well-maintained green
Secure and secluded
Commanding a prime position

Condition

Recently decorated
Immaculate condition
Excellent
Tastefully restored
Year built

Recently rewired
Pristine condition
Modern decor
Superbly presented
Quality finish throughout
Beautifully presented
In turnkey condition
Incorporating many expensive extras
Totally refurbished
Brand-new
Impeccably presented
Luxurious
Exceptional detached home
A haven of style
Spectacular four-bedroomed
In showhouse condition
Many original features
Decorated by a professional

Land and gardens

Large corner site
Mature gardens
Fruit trees
Water feature
Panoramic views
South-facing rear garden
Walled garden

Cobblelock driveway
Manicured lawn
Elevated garden
Ranch-style fencing
Stone boundary walls
About ½ acre
Private/South-facing patio area
Gardens laid to lawn
Woodland setting
Electronic access gates
Double garage
Sunny rear garden

Investment-related

Bag a bargain
Massive potential
Packaged to go
Tempting value at
Strong rental demand
Excellent investment
Great value
Priced to sell fast
Genuine value
The right price

The body of the advert should list the features of your home that will mean the most to your probable buyer. Based on the size of your home, its location and price, make a guess as to who your probable buyer is and decide which features will interest them the most. Will they have school-age children? If so, include proximity to schools in the body of your advert. Describe features of the property which will appeal to them specifically, rather than the entire public. The availability of public transport, schools, job opportunities and local shops are examples of features that translate as benefits to the buyer. Use the list of features we have included as a checklist of what you might include in the body of your advert.

Interior specifics

Gas-fired central heating
Tiled kitchen floor
Cast-iron stove
PVC windows
Surround-sound system installed
Wired for satellite television
Interior decorated
Bright living quarters
Designer bathroom
Underfloor heating
Central vacuum system

Luxury fitted wardrobes
Fitted with alarm
Integrated appliances
Number of fireplaces
Solid wood flooring
Maple kitchen
Recessed lighting
Generous proportions
Cleverly designed
Impressive entrance hall
Marble flooring
Charming and bright
Granite worktop
Balcony
CCTV system

Size

Substantial family home
Stunning and spacious
Number of rooms
Extended
Number of bathrooms
Abundance of entertaining space
Luxurious family home
Spacious family home
Square footage/metreage
Generously proportioned

Number of bedrooms
Boasts extensive living accommodation
Number of reception rooms
Deceptively large
Luxurious bedrooms

Location

Near shops and schools
Within walking distance of . . .
Popular residential location
Uninterrupted views
Easy commute
Quiet street
Near tennis courts
Near park/schools/church/shops
Centrally located
Quiet and convenient location
Waterside location
Cul-de-sac
On bus, Luas, Dart, rail route
Tranquil setting
Sought-after location
Rural setting
An abundance of amenities
Other useful phrases
Look no further!
Yours for only

The home you deserve
A beautiful home
Double-fronted
Breathtaking sea views
Upgraded
Impressive family home
Stylish and detached
Ideal trader-upper
Benefits from
Architecturally designed
Grab the good life
The best move of your life
For the opportunity of a lifetime
Waiting for you at only . . .
Stunning and spacious
It will steal your heart
Start packing!

Always give the location of the property. Buyers are interested in specific areas. They will pass over your listing if the location is omitted. After all, property is all about location, location, location. The perfect house in the wrong location won't suit potential buyers.

A missing price suggests the property is too expensive, so always include your asking price or, at the very least, a guide price.

Be sure to end your advertisement by giving the reader a reason to call, then ask them to do it. You could use one of the following phrases if appropriate:

Unbeatable value

Don't let this one get away

Act now to arrange a viewing

Bound to sell quickly

What are you waiting for?

Too good to last

Nothing like it at this price

Make this home yours

Be the proud owner

Big home, little budget

Your dreams come true

Don't compromise on quality

Viewing highly recommended

Final offers being accepted

Last chance to purchase

The perfect choice

For the alert buyer

Call today for details

Have it all; call today

Call now to view

Luxury you deserve

More for your money

Waiting for you

To see it is to want it
A unique opportunity
An excellent opportunity to acquire
Experience city living

Adverts, especially cost-effective classified adverts, should be booked to appear on a regular basis. If they are being placed in a daily paper, ensure that they run for a week or more before you decide whether they are effective or not. Always remember the golden rules of property advertising: exposure, exposure, exposure.

Selling your home is a team game, so it is in your interests to help your estate agent. You can start by telling everybody that your house is for sale. Get your estate agent to give you a few brochures and put them in waiting rooms and reception rooms wherever you go. Display the brochure for your property at work. Each bid is worth a few thousand euro to you, so if you can generate more leads and more bids, it all counts.

CHAPTER 6

DRESSED TO SELL

Your auctioneer will bring prospective purchasers to your property, but don't expect them to sell your home unaided. A saleable home speaks for itself. Each room can send out a unique message to viewers. Stimulate the buyer's imagination by setting the scene for them. If they can see themselves living 'happy ever after' in your house, you will be well on the road to obtaining a bid from them.

In this chapter, I will advise on how to prepare your home for viewings and how to examine the house internally and externally to ensure that it is presented in the best light and so ensure you receive an excellent price.

Similar to first impressions when meeting new people, the initial impression your home makes is long-lasting and is usually hard to erase. Since this is the case, it is in your best interest to display your home in the best possible light. Although we all know that it is unwise to make snap judgements, that is exactly what buyers tend to do. They will inevitably notice the paint cracks in the walls rather than the beautifully finished wood floors. Therefore, it is imperative that you take note of the imperfections in your home and take steps to correct them.

At the other extreme, some sellers make the mistake of investing a great deal into their home prior to selling in the hope of substantially increasing their selling price. Unfortunately, spending €5,000 to install a new patio in the back gardens does *not* normally translate to a €5,000 increase in your selling price. Sure, the buyer may love the fact that the house now comes complete with a brand-new deck or barbeque area, but they certainly don't want to pay an extra cent for it. Your goal is to maximise the attractiveness of your home, not to redo it entirely. A thorough cosmetic overhaul is usually all that's needed to make your home more desirable.

A lot of what needs to be done to get a home ready for the market doesn't cost much, but it does take time. As mentioned in Chapter 1, the first thing you need to do is to stop thinking of your house as 'home' and start thinking about it as a commodity that you want to sell. To be a successful seller, you must detach yourself emotionally. Be brutally honest about how it should look in order to sell for the best price, fast and with the least hassle.

Presentation is important: home-buyers are attracted to bright, clean and spacious homes. Property condition and appearance play a much bigger part in home sales now than they did in the past. Today's buyers massively discount the price if a home needs work, if they buy it at all. Most home-buyers are time-poor and cash-rich in today's busy society. Also, many people lack the skills to do even the most basic DIY jobs.

With the word out and prospective buyers lining up to see your home, now is the time to make sure your house looks its best. Never underestimate the power of a first impression. The best way to begin is to seek the advice of a trusted friend or family member, since it is often hard to be objective when it comes to your own home. Ask them for their opinions on what would detract from the house if they were a potential buyer. Invite them to walk through your house, like a buyer would. Get their opinion on how it 'shows'. Your friend must be willing to be brutally honest, but they must also have a touch of common sense. There is probably no point in asking your estate agent to do this. When you think about it, it just wouldn't be fair.

They have probably just been appointed by you, or you might still be interviewing for agents. They are not going to risk alienating you, or inadvertently insulting you, by being too honest. Of course, they will say your home is lovely as it is and that their agency will have loads of buyers.

Go through the house and fix any defects, many of which you may have lived with for years. An irony of the tidy-up-for-sale process is that most people's homes have never looked as good as they do when they are put on the market. Finish off small DIY jobs. Make sure there are no unsightly wires hanging around. Replace broken tiles and light bulbs, fix dripping taps and clear your drains. You don't have to spend a fortune preparing your home for sale. In fact, you shouldn't. Concentrate on a small number of cost-effective improvements that will give you a good return on your investment.

Your goal is to dazzle buyers. So, brighten up the house and remove all clutter from countertops, tables and rooms. Scrub down your house from top to bottom. Make it sparkle. Simple aesthetic improvements such as trimming trees, planting flowers, fixing squeaky steps, doors and broken tiles, shampooing rugs and even redecorating faded paintwork will greatly enhance the appeal of your house.

You need to declutter and depersonalise your home as much as you can. Try not to have an abundance of family photos displayed around the house. Sports trophies, collectible items and souvenirs fall into the same category. If at all possible, remove some of these items from view. Store them away neatly. This is often the hardest part for most people; unfortunately, potential buyers may view the clutter as reflective of an unkept house, or worse. Buyers should be able to see how they can put their own stamp on a property. They are attracted to clean and spacious houses, so get rid of superfluous furniture.

In order to declutter, some homeowners rent storage space if their own storage space is limited. Removing excess personal possessions and furniture is important. Buyers need to be able to see past the owner's belongings and to imagine themselves living in the house.

Re-evaluate the use of all the rooms in your house. If your house is being sold as a four-bedroom house, ensure that there is a bed in all four bedrooms. Don't leave one bedroom as an office. Buyers don't pay for offices. An extra bedroom means more money in your pocket. Let's go through your home room by room. The following lists some of the things you may want to look out for.

THE INTERIOR OF YOUR HOME

Kitchen

The kitchen is a great place to start removing clutter since it is one of the first rooms buyers will see and often serves as the centrepiece of a home. Clean the oven and all appliances. It's also time to get to work on the mildew and other grime that have been lurking in the corners. Remove grease spatters and polish fixtures and surfaces. You should also clear away most of your smaller appliances, such as toasters, food processors, carving knives, etc. It is important to clear the countertops as much as possible – the idea is to create open space to foster the feeling that there is plenty of room for all of the buyer's appliances. Empty out over-stuffed drawers and throw out those knick-knacks you never get around to using. Finally, don't forget to tackle the fridge and to clear off the magnets and notes and that gallery of children's artwork.

Bathroom

Nothing adds value like improvements to kitchens and bathrooms. So, repair leaky taps and clean around bathtubs, showers and sinks. Replace the shower curtain and bath mat and put out your best towels for all viewings. The bathroom should be clear of all cosmetics and toiletries. The easiest way to deal with this is to put essentials, as well as cleaning supplies, into plastic bins which can be stored in cabinets. That way you can get what you need when you need it. You can also stash them away again quickly when you know your home is going to be shown.

Storage

Again, the idea here is to create openness. No matter how large the built-in-wardrobe really is, if it appears crammed full, a buyer may get the impression that space is limited. On the contrary, if clothes and shoes are neatly arranged, the buyer will be impressed by how organised their space can be.

The ultimate culprit when it comes to clutter always tends to be the 'storage rooms', such as the utility room, garage or the attic. 'That's what they're meant for', we reason with ourselves. However, when selling a home, it is essential to leave these areas as empty as possible so the buyers can more easily imagine what they would do with the space. The local recycling centre and dump are well worth a visit, and remember to check out your area's Freecycle service and charity shops and auction websites such as eBay. Remember you are going to have to clear it all up before you leave anyway, so why not do it now when it will put money in your pocket by making a sale easier and your house more presentable?

Furniture

This is the most overlooked form of clutter: namely, too much furniture in not enough space. When you fit several pieces of furniture in one room for your personal living needs, it tends to shrink the size of the room. From an aesthetic standpoint, the room appears small and cramped. The less furniture you keep, the more appealing your home will be to potential home-buyers. This is the time to throw out old pieces of furniture – pieces that you don't intend taking with you when you move. Again, freecycle, the recycling centre and the dump are your friends. Go and visit them. Alternatively, rent storage space for excess property until the house is sold.

Plumbing and fixtures

Take stock of all sink fixtures throughout the house. They should all look shiny and new. A good silver polish should work wonders, but if it doesn't, you'll have to spend some money and replace the worn taps. This should be fairly inexpensive and easy to do. Look out for leaks. A simple washer replacement should do the trick in most cases. Although you may have grown accustomed to the small imperfections in your home, prospective buyers notice everything, and it will weigh heavily when they make their final decision.

Carpet and flooring

Unless your carpet appears especially old or worn, a good carpet cleaner should be all you need. A professional carpet-cleaning service will cost in the region of €200–300 to clean all the carpets in the typical family home. If there are noticeable stains or wear, however, you may want to consider replacement. Choose an inexpensive floor covering in a light, neutral colour – light colours always tend to enlarge spaces. If you have hardwood floors, think about having them refinished. This can often be done relatively easily by yourself. You may simply need to sand them and recoat them to restore their shine. Alternatively, getting in a professional will cost in the region of €200 to €400 for a typical apartment – money well spent.

Ceilings, walls and paint

Check your ceilings for water stains. If you have any, be sure to paint over them. If there are any leaks, you will have to have them repaired first. Also, examine the walls for stains or cracks. These too should be fixed and are inexpensive ways to improve the appearance of your home. In fact, an overall fresh paint job is probably your best investment when selling your home. This is particularly true if your personal decorating taste tends towards the dramatic. The chances are that a buyer will never get over the fire-engine red of the bathroom walls and the purple fittings in time to notice the Jacuzzi tub. This auctioneer once found himself trying to sell a property with one of the bedrooms painted black. The walls, the ceilings and even the carpet were soot black. I say I tried to sell it. I failed, and naturally blamed the decor for my failure!

Windows and doors

Check all windows and doors to make sure they open and close easily. If there are squeaks, a squirt of old-fashioned 3-in-one oil should help. Obviously, if there are any cracked or broken windowpanes, be sure to have them replaced prior to showing your home. Having said that, when Roy Keane's parents purchased a home off me years ago, it had two broken windows the day they viewed it. The owners' sons were obviously using the windows as hurling goals the evening before and broke two separate panes of glass. We were lucky that the future owners were not put off, probably as their own family had a sports-mad son as well.

Odours

Smokers and pet owners should take special care to remove any odours that may linger in the house prior to showing. If you are a smoker, try to make a conscious effort to smoke outside of the home while it is on the market. You can also use one of the air-freshener sprays that neutralise odours. Try carpet fresheners, potpourri or scented candles also. It is also a good idea, weather permitting, to open a few windows whenever you can and let fresh air through the house. (Be careful that excess noise from outside won't be off-putting to the viewers.) If you can, fill the house with fresh flowers when you are expecting a viewing. Ask a friend, one who doesn't smoke or have a pet, to assess your efforts.

Borrow

Don't be afraid to beg or borrow what you need from friends or family – or even to rent a couple of pieces of furniture. One or two 'prop' pieces are preferable to the ripped and stained couch your dog has spent the past three years gnawing and which the baby has been sick on. Don't ever leave a room empty. Buyers need to be able to visualise the space as usable, and you can't rely on their imagination in every case.

Cleaning

Cleanliness is next to godliness when it comes to selling homes. The interior of your home, including the windows, should gleam, and you should keep it that way during the entire marketing period. Hire a cleaning person or service to come once a week if you are a busy person who doesn't have help. Your house sale is worth it.

THE EXTERIOR OF YOUR HOME

Before a buyer steps into your house, they will form an opinion. Maintaining the exterior of your home is probably just as important a part of showcasing as is the interior. As with the interior, you get only one chance to make a first impression. Spruce up the exterior of your home. Make buyers want to see the inside. Remember that the exterior is the first thing a potential home-buyer will see from their car and can be the deciding factor as to whether or not they wish to see more.

Most auctioneers and estate agents will request that people who wish to view your home look at the property from the outside before they make an appointment to view the interior. Indeed, many buyers first come across a property when they, or a friend or relative, see the 'For Sale' sign. The way your house presents itself from the road is very important. A front gate hanging on a hinge, or peeling paint, can cause buyers to wonder what else is wrong. You want to convey the impression that your home is well maintained. As such, it is critical that the outside matches the style and grace of your home as much as possible.

Stand across the road and consider the following factors when assessing the 'drive-by' appeal of your home.

Front entrance

The entrance is key to a good first impression. The front door of the house should be especially attractive. It is the first part of the home that potential buyers will be directly exposed to up close. So, paint, clean or stain it if necessary. A newly painted front door with shiny brass fittings always goes down well. Make sure that both the light over the door and the doorbell are in working order, especially in the winter months. Replace missing house numbers and make sure the number is visible from the street. Consider putting out a welcome mat and a selection of potted plants leading up to the front door.

Don't leave your rubbish bins out all day. If you are at work, ask a neighbour or a friend to bring them in. It makes your property as well as the whole neighbourhood look better.

Lastly, make sure that the lock and the key work smoothly and easily. It gives a bad impression if the estate agent cannot get in or if they have trouble with the lock. Also, it places the agent under pressure at a time when you need them to be relaxed with the viewers and ready to perform their sales job.

Front garden

How does the front garden look? Stand on the other side of the road and assess it. Is it at least on a par with those of the surrounding neighbours? If not, visit your local garden centre and buy a few matured flowers or bushes to decorate it. Be sure to buy only matured greenery. Although the immature trees and bulbs are cheaper, you cannot afford to wait until they have grown. The grass should be neatly trimmed and free of weeds. What's wrong with cutting it twice a week for the short time it will be on the market? Flowerbeds should appear well kept and attractive, and keep all shrubs, bushes and trees trimmed.

Windows

Although it is probably your least favourite chore, you'll need to wash the windows regularly, both inside and out. Consider making a regular booking with the local window-cleaner. Sunshine gives a bright, warm light and can provide an instant pick-me-up for a dreary room. Once the windows are clean, pull back the curtains or raise up the blinds and let the sun shine in. If you have net curtains, you should take them down.

Paint

Check the exterior walls of your home to make sure they look as good as possible. Consider hiring a power washer and giving them a thorough clean. However, if the paint is peeling and chipping away, the only solution may be to repaint. You can do it yourself or hire someone, but, in the end, balance the cost of a freshly painted home against the benefits of getting it sold for the best price in the shortest time and with the least hassle.

Back garden

As with the front garden, make sure the back garden is kept tidy and neat. If there are flowerbeds, tend to them on a regular basis so they don't appear overgrown and unkempt. Also, make sure the grass on the lawn is kept neat at all times. It goes without saying that any dog run should be kept spotless of dog litter.

Neighbourhood

There may not be much that you can do with the rest of the property's surroundings, be they the neighbourhood or the street, but if there is a resident's association in place, you might ask them to help you to clean up the local area with you. If you get on very well with your neighbours, you might get them to clean up their properties too.

HOME STAGING

One of the ways to ensure that your home is sold sooner rather than later is to take part in a new trend known as 'staging'. Staging can range from simply sprucing things up to hiring a professional to come in and decorate.

There is nothing wrong with the DIY approach to staging, but if you haven't got the time or the energy, or simply don't feel confident in your fashion ability, you could get professional home stagers in to ready your home for the marketing campaign. Home-staging experts come in and declutter, depersonalise and, crucially, provide home-sellers with furniture and accessories for the duration of a sales campaign in order to enhance the presentation of the property. Such services can really come in handy in the case of unfurnished houses. There are now many professional home-staging companies, some of whom offer a full turnkey package involving gardening, painting and flower-changing also.

The practice of home staging is particularly aimed at the top-end houses which are not looking their best. Some home-staging firms claim that staging can add between 5 and 10 per cent onto the value of a house. It could well be true. Just look at any new housing development. Their show unit is always expertly 'staged'. The furniture is appropriate for the rooms. Every item matches perfectly.

While many professionals agree that giving thought to the finishing touches in your home is well worthwhile, I'm not convinced that home staging works all the time. This is especially so for a one-off sale, such as your home. It's not like when a developer or builder is selling many units based on the staging of one show unit. It can be quite expensive to get stagers in and may not be economical. It's a wonderful idea, but it does not guarantee results.

CHAPTER 7

SHOWING YOUR HOME

If you and/or your agent have done your marketing well, you will quickly find that you are converting callers into real prospects, people who wish to come to see your home. When you are selling your home, you must make it available when a potential buyer wants to see it, not necessarily when it's convenient for you. If someone wants to see it at three in the afternoon and you had planned on going out, cancel your plans and show the house. In general, you must bend over backward to make time for buyers to see the place. It's necessary if you want to sell your home. A serious buyer is looking not only at your house but also at many other houses. If your home isn't available to view, that buyer may go to see another one and possibly buy it instead of yours. In the end, the more people who see your home, the more likely you are to sell it quickly. You must ensure that you capitalise on the marketing and the time you spent on dressing your home for sale. Set the tone and make viewers feel at ease.

YOUR AGENT

Have faith in your estate agent and their ability to show your home. After all, showing the property is probably the easiest part of any estate agent's job. The hard chores are to source viewers, to persuade them to view the property and then, if they are interested, to elicit a top-class offer from them – one that will persuade you to sell.

Before any viewing of your home, your agent needs to do a few things, for both you and the potential buyers, to maximise the potential of each and every appointment. They will confirm appointments with both you and the prospective purchaser, giving as much notice as you, the seller, need. On the day of the appointment, your estate agent should arrive at least five minutes early. This helps them to be in the right frame of mind for the viewing. They will normally ensure that their mobile phone is left on silent or in the car during viewings. They will open up the house and be ready to invite the viewers in. Having copies of the property's brochures available for all viewers is also highly desirable. Finally, at the end of the viewing, they will be sure to lock up the property and leave it as they found it. Hopefully they will leave a note for you, the anxious seller, giving details on how the viewing went.

VIEWING ARRANGEMENTS

The more people that view your home, the more likely it is to attract offers and sell quickly. Be as flexible on viewing times as possible, so that you don't lose prospective purchasers. Have the house ready to show with one day's prior notice. Many viewers won't bother looking at a house that takes any longer to arrange a viewing. Your efficient estate agent will be able to ring you the day before most viewings with the times they are showing your property. With this arrangement, you can realistically have the house looking its best for prospective buyers.

But always be prepared. Sometimes your estate agent will know that they have an excellent prospect, and they will want to show your home at short notice. If at all possible, allow them to go ahead and show it. I once sold a home to a hospital consultant from out of town. The consultant flew in for a job interview in the morning – and got the job, as he expected. In the afternoon, we showed him two properties, and he bought one of them. We knew in advance that we had a committed and time-sensitive potential buyer on our hands.

Showing your home is a job that will be best done by your estate agent. There are as many different ideas as to how an estate agent should show a home as there are estate agents. Having said that, politeness and courtesy go a long way, as does the simple task of turning off their mobile phone and requesting that viewers do the same. Most importantly, the estate agent should always be knowledgeable on your property, its surrounds and its selling features.

It amazes many people that someone can make a decision to spend hundreds of thousands of euros after maybe spending only ten to fifteen minutes inside a property. But that's the property market. Even if they have a second viewing, they might not be in the property for more than a half an hour. Amazing, when you think about it, and all the more reason to ensure that the potential purchasers are made to feel comfortable when viewing your home.

ELIMINATE DISTRACTIONS

Viewers are there with a purpose – to see if they wish to bid on or, hopefully, even buy your home. It is a good idea to air out the house for an hour or so before all viewings. Opening some windows helps eliminate stuffiness or odours. This might sound mean, but children, no matter how cute you think they are, can be distracting. So have them visit a neighbour and ensure that they do not return until after the viewing. Turn off the television and the radio. Viewers are not there to be entertained. Please, please, please put pets out. It's no fun to have a potential purchaser run from a house in hysterics because they found a hamster or a snake. Even though the offending animal or reptile might be safe in its cage, it can still be extremely off-putting. Hand your pets over to a friend to mind while your home is on the market.

MAKE YOURSELF SCARCE!

When the auctioneer is showing your home, leave the house or keep out of sight. If the agent is brave enough, or honest with you, they will ask you to leave when the house is being shown. Why? Because lurking sellers make viewers extremely nervous. They don't feel comfortable inspecting somebody else's home in the first place. It is also a big decision for them, and they don't need to feel they are intruding in your personal space. Once you've answered the door and welcomed the agent, who should have arrived before the viewers, find something to do outside of the home. Visit friends, go for a walk or do the shopping, but get out of the way if at all possible. The only valid excuses for staying in are illness and infirmity.

A preferable alternative is to give your agent a key to your property and disappear even earlier so that there is no chance of encountering the potential purchasers.

No buyer, or estate agent, feels comfortable viewing a property if the seller is hovering about. Often what is putting a prospective purchaser off bidding on a property is something so minor that when they mention it, the estate agent will have an immediate answer. The problem is that this worry will not be voiced by the potential purchaser for fear of offending the seller, if they are in earshot. The potential buyer must feel free to express their concerns.

If you have to stay in the property, be as invisible as possible and say nothing unless asked a direct question.

SECURITY PRECAUTIONS

When selling privately, one thing you simply must get used to is showing your home to strangers. While there are security issues surrounding this, by being observant, cautious and smart, you can go a long way towards protecting yourself. First and most importantly, when somebody phones to arrange an appointment, get the caller's name, address and phone number. This does not ensure that the caller is a prospective buyer and does not have criminal intentions, but it helps, and it gives you the chance to call back and confirm your appointment before allowing anyone into your home.

Ensure that your children, whatever age they are, do not allow viewers into the property. Children love being helpful and might think that, as you are anxious to sell and move to another home, they should show the caller the property. Safety is not a concept that children, be they a toddler or teenager, understand.

Even when you stress on all your literature that your home is available for viewing by appointment only, people will knock on the door and ask to see it right away. Be careful: drop-ins are totally unscreened. You don't know anything about them, and you could be putting yourself at risk by letting them in.

Sometimes a person will call and simply say, 'I want to come and see your home. I can be there in ten minutes, is that OK?' A wise strategy is to ask for their name, phone number and address. If a person is willing to give an address, it often means that they are sincere about looking at your home and, perhaps, buying it.

Never let anyone drop into your house after dark. It's just too dangerous. This is a simple safety precaution. If someone has harmful intentions, they will be more inclined to carry them out in the dark when it's harder to see what's going on. Anyway, most people who view a property in the dark have to come back again in daylight to get a better look.

Never show the property when you are alone, particularly if you are a woman. Explain that it is an inconvenient time and offer to set up an appointment. Always try to have a friend or relative there with you. If it's a weekend afternoon and lots of people are around, you might consider taking a chance, but ring your neighbour or a friend and ask them to look in on you in 15 to 20 minutes' time to be safe. Take note of the viewer's car registration and leave the curtains open so people can easily see inside.

When you're setting up the appointment, try to leave yourself at least an hour for the viewing. You do not want to be rushing an interested party because you have to pick up children from school.

Once the buyers are in the house and you've established a rapport with them, think of the following as your number-one rule for showing your house: 'Get out of the buyer's way.' You can get potential buyers into your house, but you can't make them buy. The

very worst thing you can do is to point out every feature. Alternatively, the best thing you can do, after
welcoming them into your house and establishing
rapport is to leave them find their own way around.
Yes, you can walk around with them (to be sure they
don't take anything), but it's best if you let them
wander through your house and see it for themselves.
Your goal is to make the buyers feel comfortable in
your home. They need to feel that they could live in
your house and make it their own. They can't possibly
do that if you stand next to them and keep pointing
out all the ways that you've made the house your
own.

It can be great to meet the potential buyers and discuss the property with them directly rather than
through a middle man. Keep records of those who
visit, and especially of anybody who makes a credible
offer. Be sure to ring all viewers for feedback after-
wards and to see if they wish to make an offer.

AFTER THE VIEWING

An efficient estate agent will call you or leave a note
at the property to report on the viewer's reaction,
even if negative. Listen to their comments. Don't get
defensive if the agent says that the viewers were
critical of some feature: see if you can correct the

problems these viewers mentioned. Remember that selling your home is a team game, so work with your estate agent for a better result. No house is perfect. Be open to making small and inexpensive changes that could impress the next viewer. From time to time, you should meet with your estate agent and have a strategy meeting. (Beware, if you have cut their fee to the bone they may not be willing to spend the extra time with you.) Feel free to offer suggestions for selling or marketing your home more effectively. Let the agent think about the answers, and they may well be willing to change their plan of attack.

Finally, on days of viewings, do not leave bread baking in the oven or fresh coffee in the pot. You may burn down the house. Viewers only laugh at this and think that the homeowner is desperate to sell. On the other hand, ensure that the television and radio are turned down or off and that the dog and cat are not to be seen.

CHAPTER 8

METHODS OF SALE

There are three alternative ways of offering your home – or any property for that matter – for sale. They are:

1. private treaty
2. public auction
3. tender.

The method of sale used by your auctioneer will depend on the character of your property as well as your needs and plans.

A good auctioneer will give advice on the method of sale, and the decision normally depends on the characteristics of the property, the state of the market and the client's requirements. Sometimes, a seller wants a quiet sale. If so, an auction with its attendant extra publicity is certainly not an option. When there is a contentious separation case, a contested will or bad feelings between two or more vendors, an auction will often be the chosen method of sale, as all dealings are in public. A private tender is seldom used for homes.

PRIVATE TREATY

This is by far the most common method of selling residential property in Ireland. An asking or guide price is placed on the property, and negotiations are conducted with interested parties, leading to a successful sale. The guide price is decided by you, the seller, in conjunction with, and taking into account, the opinions and advice you have received from your auctioneer. The chosen auctioneer puts up the 'For Sale' sign, makes out a brochure for the property and starts selling. Any agreement is normally 'subject to contract', which basically means that either party can back out of the deal until contracts are signed.

The advantages of selling by private treaty are that details of the exact sales price can be kept confidential. The fact that bidding can be made conditional on certain facts, such as survey or loan approval, encourages people to bid without having to incur expense.

Selling by private treaty is a relatively open-ended method. What I mean by this is that the property stays on the market until such time as a bidder makes an offer that is acceptable to you. In a strong market, this can be immediate, i.e., less than a week. In a slower market, it can take months, or even years. In southern Spain in 2007, the average time that a second-hand property was on the market before it was sold was three years.

In the event that the property encourages exceptionally keen interest at a particular price level, the auctioneer may suggest a private auction (the bidders are invited to attend an auction, where the property will be sold to the highest bidder) or a closed tender (the bidders are invited to provide a written or verbal bid on a 'best and final offer' basis within a given time frame).

Selling by private treaty is to be recommended for most property sales. It will realise the best price in the least time, with the least hassle for you, the owner, for the majority of properties. Marketing costs are normally less for disposal by private treaty than either public auction or tender.

PUBLIC AUCTION

It is said in the property world that an auction is a great way to sell and a horrible way to buy a home. The auction method is where potential buyers publicly bid against each other up to and beyond the reserve price. Public auctions work extremely well for properties with special characteristics which are likely to attract considerable demand. They are not to be recommended for more standard properties. Your home should be offered for sale by auction only if it is likely to attract significant demand.

A public auction involves a marketing campaign of between three and six weeks. The advantages of the auction system for a vendor are that there is a concentrated sales effort and a set date for selling. This will crystallise competitors for the property and, hopefully, maximise the price.

An auction can be stressful as you have to commit to a marketing campaign and you have no bids during this period by which to gauge interest. Once the property is sold, a purchaser normally pays a 10 per cent deposit on the auction day, and closing is normally twenty-eight days to a month later.

Auctions are great because they are final. If a bid is successful, the bidder signs contracts there and then and must go through with the purchase.

Auction tactics

Don't be surprised at an auction for your home if somebody, often a solicitor or other auctioneer acting for a prospective purchaser, asks awkward questions about the legal title to your home or claims that some wayleaves (rights of way) are not in order. It is a standard trick, used by some interested parties. They are doing it in the hope of unnerving some other potential bidders in the auction room and putting them off making a bid. If your solicitor has assured you that the property's title is in order, trust them. I have often been employed to act as a devil's advocate and disrupt auctions in this way. It's part of the game.

One of the most important pieces of advice I can give anybody who intends selling or, for that matter, buying, a property by auction is that they should make a point of attending some other auction beforehand. Get a feel for what happens, for what games are played, and view at close quarters how the excitement affects people differently. Books, films and television shows more often than not do not convey a true picture of the pressure involved in an auction situation. It's not like you are James Bond, or some other special agent, buying a rare artefact at an auction at Sotheby's. Not at all.

Auctions are 100-per-cent transparent and are proof that the market value has been obtained. For this reason, trustees, liquidators and executors often use this method. Put simply, if there is a possibility of conflict, an auction provides little reason for complaint, as anybody who turns up on the day of the auction can buy the property.

Should you sell before the auction?

There's no doubt that there is a lot of nervousness in auction rooms. Some potential buyers seek to avoid that. It is always open to prospective buyers to make a pre-auction offer, through your selling agent, but it's relatively rare that these are accepted. Experienced estate agents are well used to interested parties suggesting a pre-auction purchase. They do so in an attempt to get a bargain, which just about never happens. This is for a number of reasons, not least because you, the seller, often feel you will get a better price at the auction.

Of course, a viewer could make an offer that you can't refuse on the first day of viewings. But a more realistic scenario is that they will wait until the week of the auction and put in an offer then. At that point, your estate agent will know how the campaign is going. They will know, for example, how many (or if any) conditions of sale have gone out. They will also have a fairly good idea of who is going to turn up on auction day. The estate agent will put any realistic offer to the seller, accompanied with their opinion of that offer. If you decide to accept the offer, ensure that the bidder pays a non-refundable deposit of 10 per cent and signs binding contracts before the auction is cancelled.

However, if you are not happy with the offer, you can always say, 'No thanks, we'll see you in the auction rooms', as, in all probability, if the bidder is sufficiently interested, they will be there.

Who's showing up?

Prior to an auction, potential bidders will have done a few things to signify their interest. They will, obviously, have viewed the property, once, twice or possibly more often. They will probably have arranged for an engineer to examine the property and will almost certainly have had their solicitor request a copy of the title to the property from your solicitor.

The latter is the most important indicator to an astute estate agent of the level of interest and the number of bidders one can expect to have at an auction. If your solicitor has had four or five requests for contracts and copies of title deeds, it is safe to assume that there will be competition in the auction room and, hopefully, an excellent price and a sale.

What if only one bidder shows up? This is where you find out how good your auctioneer really is. We once conducted an auction where we knew that only one set of title deeds were issued. Furthermore, given the type of property and its location, there was only one possible bidder and potential purchaser (the neighbour). Yet, we made our reserve price, with a bit to spare, and the sellers were extremely happy. It was probably the hardest day's auctioneering I have ever had. The auction was, naturally, a flop, but by negotiating with the potential purchaser and utilising experience, possibly more akin to horse-trading or haggling over an item at a Spanish market stall rather than your conventional picture of auctioneering, the property was sold.

The sellers could hardly believe that their property was sold for an amount more than twice the highest, and only, bid at auction. We were lucky, but we also had a contingency plan, given that only one set of title deeds had been requested. One of my colleagues that day had thirty years' auctioneering experience. That experience and the aforementioned horse-trading is what saved the day and clinched the sale.

Setting the guide price

The auctioneer does not know that bidding will exceed the advised minimum value or guide price. They might hope that it does. They might wish and pray that it does, but they do not know that it will. I recently held a private auction for a small plot of land which I valued at about €350,000. The vendor wanted €400,000. We had been selling the property by private treaty when bidding went to €400,000. We stopped taking bids at this stage and invited the three bidders and anybody else who had requested details to an auction in a hotel.

Remember, the owners were happy with €400,000. We told everybody who was invited this, and if there was no bid over €400,000 the owners were quite willing to sell for this amount. It was the reserve. The bidding came thick and fast as soon as the auction began. I had to constantly pinch myself to avoid smiling, although I must admit that I couldn't suppress a grin when bidding went above €1 million. It slowed down then, and the land subsequently sold for about €1.2 million. This was three times the owner's expectations and the reserve.

So, guide prices are not always purposely set low despite the final results of auctions and despite what a property-obsessed press blessed with hindsight might say.

Dutch auctions

A 'Dutch auction' has been described as being like a crab going backwards. What is meant by this is that bidding goes backwards from an initial high price quoted by the seller or their auctioneer. The seller slowly lowers his or her price, waiting for the first and only bid which will seal the sale. There is obviously no need for a second bid, as it can only be for a lower amount. The property is secured by the first bidder.

I have never seen or heard of an example of a Dutch auction. Neither have I met, nor do I expect to meet, anybody who has. In a way, the modern equivalent is a tender process. This is where potential purchasers make sealed bids without knowing what amount their rivals are willing to pay for the property. If you bid too low, you don't get the property. If you bid too high, you get the property but often will wonder if you have paid too much.

Even if a sale is not realised at the auction, all is not lost. Often property sells immediately after the auction by negotiation.

Negotiating after auction

By looking into their eyes, by seeing the sweat on their brows and palms of their hands, by nervous twitches or glancing looks from one to another, an experienced auctioneer knows when potential purchasers are at their limit. It is for all the world like a high-stakes poker game, and, like in Las Vegas, the nervous telltale signs are evident.

This is especially so in 'after the auction' negotiating. The bidders/potential purchasers have been nervously waiting for the auction time; they probably arrived extra early to ensure that they would be on time; they have discussed possible strategies at length with each other and with their solicitor. They have endured an auction. They have held their nerve and are the highest bidder, but the auctioneer won't bring down the hammer and close the deal as the owner still won't sell. They are still in the game, but the match is going into extra time. The seller's auctioneer is exclusively dealing with them to see if a deal can be reached. Will this be their new home or not?

As an auctioneer, it's great. We have all the advantages. So, really, I'm not being cocky in saying that the auctioneer has all the aces in an auction situation – for a residential property. Trust your professional advisers, both your solicitor and your auctioneer. Listen to their ideas and reasoning. Utilise their experience and advice. This will ensure the maximum chances of a successful outcome.

SALE BY TENDER

A sale by tender has many of the characteristics of a sale by auction. There is a three- to six-week advertising campaign. Potential buyers have to ensure that engineer's reports and title details are in order. The unusual thing about sale by tender is that no asking price is quoted. Interested parties make up their own mind on what value to place on the property. It is a seldom-used method, and only properties with unique, hard-to-value features – often commercial properties – are suited to this.

In reality, private treaty is the most common method of sale. To recap, this means that the auctioneer puts up a 'For Sale' sign, negotiates with interested parties and, when a price is agreed, a contract is drawn up and signed by both parties. This is normally the best way to sell your home quickly and for the most money.

CHAPTER 9

UNDERSTANDING OFFERS

Just as you have a selling price in mind, potential buyers have a figure in their mind. When you receive an offer, either directly, if selling privately, or via your auctioneer, you can either choose to accept it, reject it or make a counter-offer and negotiate the price. Depending on the strength of the market, counter-offers can go back and forth a few times via your estate agent.

Clearly, you are looking to sell for as much as possible, while the buyer is trying to get the best deal from their point of view (that is, to buy a suitable home for the best price for them). Some negotiating is required to ensure that everyone walks away from the transaction satisfied. Successful negotiations are highly dependent on reasonable expectations on the seller's part as well as a certain degree of finesse and people skills on the part of the negotiator – usually, the estate agent.

There are a number of things to keep in mind. A crucial sticking point in negotiation is separating the emotional aspect of the sale from the financial one. It's easy to let personal feelings or emotions get in the way of trying to agree a price. The buyer can't possibly understand all the memorable times shared in your home or the milestones celebrated there. Accordingly, they don't perceive the value of the house in the same way that you do. The purchase of your property is a financial decision for them. You don't need to like the buyer or to develop a close relationship with them. Chances are that you won't ever see them again once the sale has closed. However, it is essential not to take a low offer or a perceived slight the wrong way. If they have made an offer, they are clearly interested in purchasing your home, and their offer needs to be considered on its own merits. You do not want to do anything that might cause the potential buyer to reconsider their offer for, as many experienced auctioneers will say, 'you can only sell your home when you have an offer'.

GETTING AN OFFER AND NEGOTIATING FOR MORE

When you get an offer, don't get all excited and make a rash decision. Think things out rationally. Discuss the offer with your estate agent. Ensure that your estate agent has all of the bidder's details, including name, address and telephone (home and mobile), and knows whether the offer is subject to mortgage approval or the sale of a property.

How you judge an offer depends on market conditions and how close the bid is to your expected sale price. If you feel that the offer is sufficient, accept it. You can only sell a property when you have a valid bid. It's as simple as that. Tell your agent to take a deposit and instruct your solicitor to issue contracts.

The purchase price isn't everything. Carefully consider what the bid is conditional upon (for example, mortgage approval, engineer's report, sale of the bidder's current property). If in doubt, ask. Never be afraid to ask. It's your property and your sale. Too many contingencies can leave loopholes and cause a deal for the sale of your home to collapse.

Rarely is the first offer from anybody the absolute highest price that they are willing to pay. This applies to property as much as it applies to everything else in life. Remember that leather handbag you haggled over at the market on holidays last year or your last trip to a car-boot sale? Negotiating is as much a part of the home-buying and -selling process as it is at a market stall. Each additional €1,000 you are offered is

€1,000 in your pocket. It is here that you need to heed the advice of an experienced estate agent – or where you pay dearly for picking the wrong one.

A WARNING ABOUT DIRECT CONTACT WITH BIDDERS

If you have employed an estate agent, it is normally in your best interests not to contact or engage potential viewers, bidders or buyers. Always refer them back to your estate agent. I have found through the years that the overriding reason why bidders give an offer directly to vendors is that they hope they can purchase the property for less off you than if they go to the estate agent. Maybe they will know you indirectly through a relation or a friend. In reality, they see you as a soft touch.

However, realistically, you have appointed an estate agent to market your property and to negotiate a sale on your behalf. They are being paid anyway, so it is rather defeating the purpose not to utilise their expertise when dealing with offers and negotiating a purchase price. They have got the fish on the line; they deserve to reel it in. Your estate agent will, in all probability, be entitled to their agreed fee anyway.

CONDITIONS ATTACHED TO BIDS

Don't let greed blind you into accepting the highest offer if there are conditions attached. Sometimes a lesser monetary offer can be the better deal for you. Out of all property sales, somewhere between 3 and 5 per cent are made to people who were not the highest monetary bidder. This can lead to complaints from disgruntled potential buyers to the auctioneer's institute about your agent. But it is your decision as to which bid is best for you and which bid, if any, to accept. Your agent acts for you, so they will do their best to agree the sale with whichever buyer you choose.

As a seller, you are not obliged to accept the highest, or any, offer. Indeed, the highest offer may not be best because of conditions attached to it – for example, an offer that is subject to the sale of the buyer's own property should not be viewed as being equal to an offer free of such a condition. Even if it is at the same, or perhaps even a marginally higher, price level, it is a much weaker offer. Similarly, an offer from an individual who has already paid out money for an engineer's report on your property will be viewed as stronger than one from anyone else.

Normally, property sales are subject to title, contract, engineer's reports, mortgage approval and, sometimes, the sale of the purchaser's property. Before you accept an offer and take your property off the market, your agent should be able to assure you that the buyer can and will, in all probability, go through with the purchase.

HAS YOUR POTENTIAL PURCHASER MONEY?

Although it may appear obvious, you need to make sure your buyer is financially capable of purchasing your home. Many anxious house-owners and inexperienced estate agents waste precious time by having an unqualified buyer tie up their house with a contract that will never be signed. If a buyer is not pre-approved for a mortgage and makes an acceptable offer on your home, be sure to get written confirmation that the mortgage is in place prior to agreeing a sale. Keep trying to sell until they can produce a mortgage-approval certificate. They will produce this more speedily if they know that you are continuing to show your property and may accept rival bids until this is produced.

If your buyer claims to be pre-approved for their mortgage, you might check that your estate agent has seen a copy of their preliminary mortgage-approval certificate. It is essential that any bidder can back up their bid with money; otherwise, you are wasting your time. This approval is not binding, but if the prospective buyer cannot produce a mortgage-approval certificate, you might be better off dealing with somebody else. After all, in this day and age, banks, building societies and mortgage brokers all provide a fast and hassle-free way for prospective purchasers to obtain approval.

The valuer's report

Your purchaser's mortgage lender will order a valuation of your home to make sure they are not lending more than the house is worth. They may also order a survey to make sure that the property boundaries are properly laid out. This is normally confirmed by the purchaser's engineer, so it is not a job for you to be concerned with.

Never issue a contract to a buyer who can't get a mortgage. In the worst case, your home is tied up for a period of time while they shop around for a mortgage. Put the onus and incentive on the purchaser. As soon as they can show your agent a copy of their mortgage approval, you can take a deposit. This gives them an incentive to move fast in case somebody else beats their offer.

A good estate agent makes sure that prospective

buyers are financially qualified before they submit a bid to you. So, don't be afraid to ask your estate agent questions about the buyers' financial circumstances.

A SALE CONTINGENT ON THE SALE OF THE POTENTIAL BUYER'S OWN HOME

Unless your property is being sold to a first-time buyer, your purchaser may have to sell their current home before they can commit to yours. This is an area that often causes dispute if not handled profession-ally. Solutions to this depend on the state of the market at the time, along with the demand for your particular property.

If you do accept an offer that is subject to the sale of somebody else's property, be sure to set a time limit on how long you will wait. You should also note that they may not be in a position to sign contracts even when their property is sale agreed but will have to wait until their solicitor receives unconditional signed contracts for their sale.

It is always advisable for purchasers to have their own property on the market, if not sale agreed or sold before they look to buy, but this is not always the case. They are caught in a 'Catch-22' type of situation. They do not want to sell until they know what they are buying but are not in a position to buy until they sell. Ensure that you don't get caught out by being the solution to their problems. In most cases, it is advisable to keep your property on the market until your bidders have received a deposit on theirs. You might even get a higher bid in this time. Even when they have a sale agreed, there are no guarantees, as they might still not sign contracts on your home.

Be aware that if you take your property off the market while these bidders are attempting to sell their property, you are placing your faith not only in your prospective purchaser but also on their estate agent's ability to sell their current property. That same agent may be one whom you rejected as not being good enough to sell your property. Do you want to place your faith in them now?

Never consider your home to be sold under these circumstances. You cannot depend on a bidder who cannot buy. At the very least, give them strict time limits for selling their own property and signing unconditional contracts on yours.

SALE SUBJECT TO AN ENGINEER'S REPORT

Engineer's reports are the top deal-breakers. Should there be a major problem with your property, ask the potential purchasers for a copy of the report or, alternatively, get an engineer's report yourself. Some property commentators recommend that sellers of older homes undertake an engineer's report prior to putting the property on the market. While this can be a good idea, it must be accompanied by a commitment to rectify any problems that arise on foot of the report.

But, engineers can differ on their findings, and an engineer for the purchaser might just come up with a different set of faults requiring solutions on top of the ones you have already undertaken. Either way, be sure to see if any of the problems discovered are covered by your home insurance. Whether the problems are covered by your insurance or not, you need to consider getting the work done in order to get the best price for your home.

To explain how peculiar the wording of engineer's reports can be, I'll give you an example of which I have first-hand knowledge. A few years ago, we agreed a sale on a three-year-old house. We foresaw no potential problems with the engineer's report, as the home was still covered by the original homebond ten-year, new-home guarantee. The purchasers, when they received the report, were alarmed and threatened to pull out of the sale. The engineer had practically condemned the home. It was, according to him, 'not built in compliance with building regulations', along with a host of other minor problems. When we told the sellers, they were naturally alarmed. They sourced the original engineer's report from when they bought the property. Remember, this was only three years previously. Guess what? It was by the same engineer, and although he was now advising the potential purchasers that the house was 'not built in compliance with building regulations', he had given it a glowing report only three years previously. When confronted with these two conflicting reports, what did he say? 'Building regulations have changed since the first report'. There was nothing wrong with the house per se, except that building regulations had changed, as they do constantly. I was furious. He had put the purchasers off the property, and the sale fell through. All because building regulations had changed. If he had said that the property was built in compliance with the regulations when it was built but not now, as the regulations are constantly being upgraded, the sale would have been fine. (See Chapter 12, 'Troubleshooting', pp. 161–2 for more on engineer's reports.)

CASH DEALS

What do you do if you are offered some element of cash in an offer of your desired sales price? Say, €5,000 or €10,000, or even €50,000? Usually, the prospective purchaser wishes to keep the house below a stamp-duty threshold and, therefore, save themselves some stamp duty. You might both agree that it is a penal and unjust tax. On these grounds, you accept some cash 'under the counter'. This does happen, but it is totally illegal. In essence, it is defrauding Revenue – the taxman. Anybody involved, or anybody who even has knowledge about any 'cash under the counter' deals, is liable to a jail sentence. In fact, if your auctioneer or solicitor even suspect that there is an 'under the counter' cash payment involved in the sale, they will move very fast to distance themselves from it. Why should they go to jail for something somebody else does?

There is, on the face of it, no benefit for you, a home-seller, as there is no tax on a capital gain or profit made from the sale of your principal private residence. There can, of course, be a minor incentive when selling a second home or an investment property, as these capital gains are taxed. But, again, it is illegal, and the Revenue Commissioners will eventually come knocking. Furthermore, with the risk of money-laundering, it is even more imperative that one doesn't get involved in deals that involve cash payments. You don't know where the money came from. That mild-mannered bidder may well be a major criminal. Who would want to be accused of facilitating a drug dealer or a criminal gang of laundering their ill-gotten gains? Somebody will go to jail for it soon. Don't let it be you.

HANDING OVER POSSESSION

Sometimes it might suit both parties that you, the seller, rent the property from the purchaser for a few months after closing. It might be that you have not yet decided on where you are moving. There might be a delay in the house you are to purchase, or the house you are having built may not be ready for a few months. This might be more important to you than the last few thousand euro.

DEPOSITS ON YOUR PROPERTY

When you decide to accept an offer on your property, your estate agent will get the potential buyer to forward on a deposit to them (you *have* checked that their bond and insurances are in place?). A typical deposit on a property is in the region of 3–5 per cent of the purchase price of a second-hand property. Deposits in this country are not binding but are an act of good faith. All deposits are normally held by the estate agent as 'stakeholders pending completion of contracts'. If you have been selling your home yourself, it is a good idea to get your solicitor to hold such a deposit. Again, they should do so as 'stakeholders pending completion of contracts'.

The deposit must be returned in full should the purchaser decide not to sign the contracts, no matter what the reason. Your estate agent has no discretion over this. (Some vendors feel that as the potential purchaser has wasted their time, the agent should deduct money from the deposit, but this cannot be done.) Should the sale not proceed for any reason, your auctioneer should check to ensure that contracts and title deeds have been returned to your solicitor before refunding the deposit.

TO ACCEPT OR TO REJECT?

To summarise, after reviewing an offer on your property, you have two options: you either accept the offer, or you reject it. If the offered price is less than what you wanted, look at the offer as a whole. Be objective about the cost of holding out for more. If you are paying €1,000 per month on bridging finance, selling for €2,000 less than originally desired might be better than holding out for two months. Remember also that price is not the only negotiating point.

One thing to remember when selling your home is that you can sell your property only when you have an offer. That offer needs to be from somebody who has the finance to go through with the purchase. So, any time you have such an offer, the decision is up to you as to whether to accept it. There may, or may not, be another offer as good as the one on the table.

Don't be afraid to accept your first offer. If you've done your homework, appointed a good agent and spruced up the property, it may well happen that you receive an excellent offer in the first week of viewings. Instead of rejoicing over their good fortune, many sellers get greedy and reject the offer. Their attitude is, 'If we got that in the first week, we're sure to get more by leaving the property for sale for longer'. Don't be foolish. Discuss every offer with your estate agent. Sometimes the first offer is the best you are going to get as that person may have been waiting for a house just like yours for a while. They may appreciate what your home has to offer to them and want it badly. Many a seller has rejected an early offer and had to accept a lesser one, months down the line.

If all has gone to plan, well done! Your property is now 'sale agreed'. Your estate agent will forward details of the purchaser, their solicitor, the sales price and the amount of the deposit to your solicitor for preparing contracts and issuing them to the purchaser's solicitor.

CHAPTER 10

THE LEGAL ASPECTS

As soon as you decide to sell your home, you need to decide which solicitor to use. This can be the same solicitor as when you first bought your home or, of course, you may decide to change. There is no need to use the same one if you were not happy with their service.

Legally speaking, a contract for the sale of property, land or houses must be evidenced in writing. In essence, a note containing three key facts relating to the agreed sale – the address of the property, the price and the details of the purchaser and seller – is a contract. But legal advice is essential to ensure a smooth sale, and contracts should be issued by your solicitor. All letters and notes detailing the sale must contain the words 'subject to contract/contract denied'. Otherwise, they may inadvertently constitute a binding contract. The following is a step-by-step guide to the legal side of selling your home.

THE TITLE DEEDS

For your solicitor to prepare properly in advance for your sale, they need your authority to collect your title deeds, as these are normally held by a financial institution.

On receipt of written authority and instructions from you, your solicitor will request your title deeds from your bank or building society. This is sometimes called 'taking up your deeds'. You should insist that your solicitor obtains your title deeds immediately – as soon as your house is put on the market. Often they wait until they have received the letter of sale from your estate agent, which can cause unnecessary delays.

Obtaining the deeds to your property takes approximately two weeks, although some financial institutions are taking much longer. By obtaining your title deeds in a timely fashion, your solicitor can rectify any problems and can issue contracts of sale and title documents swiftly upon you or your estate agent agreeing a sale.

If the solicitor did not act for you when you purchased the property, they should examine the deeds to ensure that all is in order to ensure a smooth sale. If all is not in order, they should obviously take steps to rectify this on your behalf, prior to a sale being agreed.

Legal title to property in Ireland may be freehold or leasehold. Freehold is basically where the property is essentially held for ever, free of any rent. Alternatively, the title may be leasehold. Leasehold property may be for anything from 250 years to 999 years subject to a reserved (normally modest) ground rent payable to a superior titleholder. With this type of title, most leaseholders are empowered with a right to compulsorily buy out the freehold title. It is particularly important that this right be exercised well before the expiration date (called the reversion date) of the lease. Financial institutions normally refuse to lend for a property which has less than seventy-five years remaining on its leasehold.

When your solicitor reviews the deeds, if the title is 'land registry', they should obtain an up-to-date 'folio and title plan' from the Land Registry showing the title and lands and the fact that you are the registered owner of same. Some solicitors are over-particular when it comes to the title deeds. I was once selling an older property. When the contracts were sent out, the purchasers rang me in a panic and declared that the vendor's title was defective. When I enquired further, it transpired that there was a document transferring the property from one seller to another which was not correctly signed. While you might agree that this is indeed a problem, wait until I tell you the year that sale took place: 1848. The purchaser's solicitor scared off the purchasers by claiming that the title was defective because a document dated 1848 was not correctly signed and witnessed. The property had been through six different owners since then, with no problems.

I asked the purchasers, rather flippantly I suppose, if they were really concerned at the possibility that a 170-year-old person was going to turn up, knock on their door and look for his property back. They were not amused. Their solicitor had created such a totally irrational fear in their minds about the property's title that they pulled out of the purchase. It was their loss, as this old gem of a property was resold very soon after for even more money, and the original potential purchasers missed out on their dream period house.

To the best of my knowledge, no 170-plus-year-old person has yet knocked on the door claiming back their property. I think I can safely say that if a 170-year-old arrives at any of our front doors, they can have the property lock, stock and barrel, even without producing any title deeds.

LETTER OF SALE

Except for obtaining your deeds, all is quiet on the legal front until a sale is agreed and your estate agent issues the 'letter of sale' to your solicitor. This 'letter of sale' will include the price, conditions of sale, the contents included in the sale (if any), the purchaser's name and address, their solicitor's details and, sometimes, the estimated closing date. It needs to contain the words 'subject to contract', as previously mentioned.

THE CONTRACT

The contract for sale is then drawn up, assuming your solicitor has received all the relevant documentation from you and the lending institution. If the solicitor is preparing a contract for a sale by auction, they leave the purchaser's name and purchase price blank until the auction is over and the purchaser's details are known. If the sale is by private treaty, the contract will contain all names, the price and a copy of the title deeds of your property.

The engineer's report

Most sales are subject to the purchaser being happy with an engineer's report on your property. Even if the purchaser says that they do not require one, their solicitor or bank will often insist that one is done. We discuss engineer's reports in more detail in Chapters 9 and 12.

Planning permission

Any house built since October 1964 requires planning permission. Your solicitor will need to make sure that the planning documentation is in order. This will usually entail an architect's certificate stating that the conditions attached to the grant of planning permission have been respected. If there has been any development on the property since construction, a similar approval will be required.

It is very important that the planning documents are in order before the proposed sale is agreed. Otherwise, the potential purchaser may, on discovery of a discrepancy, pull out of the transaction at a very late stage. This is because most lenders will not allow them to borrow using a property as collateral which is not in compliance with the planning regulations. At very best, you will have to get retrospective planning permission for the alterations. (This is called retention.) In most cases, this is a formality but one which takes three to four months and so has the potential to delay or derail your sale.

Signed contracts returned

When the prospective purchaser's solicitor has studied the contracts and is happy with them, their client (your purchaser), if proceeding with the purchase, will sign them. This can take any length of time from a short few days to a number of weeks. The return of signed contracts means that the purchaser is ready, willing and able to proceed. They return the contract, along with the contract deposit, to your solicitor. This contract deposit is normally 10 per cent of the purchase price, less the amount they have already paid to your estate agent. A closing date is normally agreed at this time also.

The purchaser's solicitor will also order a title search to determine if there are any liens against your property. (A lien is a charge registered against the property in respect of a debt that needs to be repaid.) These tasks are the responsibility of the buyer's solicitor. All you need to do is ensure that your auctioneer encourages the purchaser to arrange that the reports are done in a timely manner.

Contracts signed by you

Your solicitor will then call on you to come into their office and sign the contract in duplicate. This is the stage at which you become legally bound to the sale.

If you are selling your family home (even if the title is in only one of the couple's names), the consent of the other spouse is required. This is required under the Family Home Protection Act 1976. If both names are on the deeds, then the problem does not arise, as both signatures are required anyway. On completion of the sale of the family home, both spouses will have to sign a Family Home Protection Act declaration. You will also have to produce a copy of your state marriage certificate.

Signing the deed and handing over the keys

The transfer or conveyance is the formal document that transfers your legal interest to the purchasers. It is signed by you in your solicitor's office and is then held on file until the closing date. You should also provide your solicitor with a set of keys and the alarm code which will be handed over on completion of the sale.

Contracts exchanged

When you have signed the contracts, your solicitor returns one copy to the purchaser's solicitor, thus completing the full exchange of contracts. This creates a binding agreement between both parties, subject to the terms and conditions set out in the contract.

Your solicitor replies to the questions raised in the requisitions by the purchaser's solicitor and returns any documents required together with written replies. They then approve the draft purchase deed and prepare the documents for closing. If there is a mortgage on the property, your solicitor will obtain redemption figures from your lending institution. The redemption figure is the amount required to redeem (pay off in full) your mortgage. This will be calculated to the scheduled closing date. Your solicitor will obtain the redemption figures from your financial institution. A full account of this will be available to you. You (and your spouse if necessary) will sign the closing documents and declarations. On closing, your solicitor will meet the buyer's solicitor and exchange the title documents and the keys of the property, which you will have provided, for the purchase money.

Issuing contracts quickly and encouraging the purchaser to sign them speedily is the only way to ensure that your sale won't fall through. The faster your solicitor issues contracts, the less time the purchaser has to change their mind. Your sale is important, to you. It is vital to get the prospective purchaser legally committed as soon as possible.

It is imperative to keep in constant communication with your solicitor to ensure that they are doing their part to move your home from being 'sale agreed' to 'sold'. While your estate agent's scope for assisting the sale after solicitors have been instructed is limited, they should also keep a check on the legal process until unconditional contracts are signed.

Completion

The sale is normally completed by the purchaser's solicitor attending your solicitor's office and handing over the balance of the purchase monies in exchange for the title deeds and possession of the property for the new owners. With the advent of more modern methods, some solicitors send the money by electronic transfer to the selling solicitor's account. The vendor's solicitor gives an undertaking (a promise) to forward the required documents to the purchaser's solicitor. They do so as soon as they have confirmation that the money is in their account. Your solicitor will confirm the closing date with you and with the purchaser's solicitor.

You must empty your house and leave it in a tidy fashion early on the completion date.

BUYING AND SELLING AT THE SAME TIME

This can be quite a tricky area if you are trying to orchestrate both to happen at the same time. It is very important to consult your solicitor as they will have experience in such matters. It is usually best to get first a binding contract for the sale of your current house. You may want to sign the contract for the purchase of the new house contingent on the sale of your old house going through. It is often not necessary that both sales close on the same day, as bridging finance can normally be arranged for a limited time period when you have unconditional contracts signed on your home.

MORTGAGE REDEMPTION AND CAPITAL-GAINS DECLARATIONS

Your mortgage is paid off from the sale proceeds by your solicitor. Your solicitor will account to you for the sale proceeds immediately following the closing of the sale. They will usually deduct their fee and associated costs (such as land-registry charges and other outlays) from the balance.

If the property is your main residence, then you are not liable for capital-gains tax. If you are selling a house which is not your main residence, then you must pay this tax. Again, your solicitor can assist you in calculating the amount that you will have to pay to Revenue, which will depend on the value of the house. Your solicitor will have to get a capital-gains tax certificate for the purchase price if the purchase price is greater than the threshold set by Revenue. They will need your personal public service (PPS) number to do this.

It is important to note that capital-gains tax is a self-assessment tax, and it is up to you to make declarations on this and to pay the correct amount. Penalties for evasion are severe.

APARTMENT SALES

In the sale of an apartment, the purchaser's solicitor will generally raise pre-contract queries specific to the sale of a property where there is a management company in place. These queries must be replied to by the management company or, more particularly, the managing agents employed by the management company to professionally manage the complex. It is essential that your solicitor be provided with the full contact details of the management agency to enable them to obtain the necessary information speedily. The managing agent will generally charge a fee for the replies to these queries. (See Chapter 11 for more on apartment sales and property-management companies.)

If the purchasers are obtaining a mortgage, like most people, their bank must be provided with proof that they have insurance on the property with the name of the purchaser and the bank written on the policy schedule. The original of this will be needed to enable the purchaser to draw down their loan. This must also be furnished by the managing agent.

Finally, on the completion of the sale, an adjustment must be made for the yearly apartment-block service charge. For example, if the service charge has been paid up until the end of the year, then the purchaser must refund the balance to the vendor of the difference. Alternatively, if the service charge is outstanding, then the vendor's solicitor has to discharge this amount out of the proceeds of the sale, up until the date of completion, and forward a copy of this receipt to the purchaser's solicitor.

SELLING AN EX-LOCAL-AUTHORITY OR AFFORDABLE HOME

In the late 1980s, early 1990s and up to the present day, local-authority tenants were and are entitled to buy their council/corporation house. These properties are normally sold to the occupier at a discount to the open-market value. The value of this discount depends on various factors, including how long it has been occupied by the tenant who is now the prospective purchaser. Most people, when they buy, don't realise that the local authority puts conditions on this sale to their sitting tenant, and this can affect matters when an ex-local-authority house is being sold on later.

The main conditions, while worded differently in many parts of the country are generally as follows:

1. The seller must obtain the consent of the local authority when selling. This is always granted subject to the local authority being satisfied that the seller has made provision for their future housing needs (that is, plans, and can afford, to buy again) and will therefore not require to be rehoused by the local authority.

2. The local authority will also insist that the first purchasers (though not subsequent purchasers) who are not local-authority tenants are not investors. The local authority's consent will not be granted if the purchasers have other property and, therefore, do not require this property as their home.

There are many forms to be filled out, both by you the vendor and the purchaser. Sales of ex-local-authority homes can take about a month longer than other homes to clear the legal process. It therefore does no harm to ask a local councillor to make representations on your behalf to speed up the process.

Properties bought under the 'affordable housing' initiative are a similar animal in a number of ways. If you are lucky enough to have purchased an 'affordable' home, you will know that it was purchased at a price below the full market value. If sold within twenty years, there is a clawback mechanism, which means that, depending on how long one has owned the property, the state or local authority will be entitled to part of the profits you have made, based on the percentage under the market price for which you purchased the property. This is only fair and, at this early stage, is being enforced.

CONVEYANCING CAVEAT

A new category of problems with getting contracts for the sale of your property signed and sales closed has arisen in the past few years. At present, some solicitor's franchises are offering conveyancing for a set low fee. The competence of these solicitors is not in question. What is a problem is that some of these solicitors have become busier than they could have possibly ever imagined. Consequently, they are so overrun that their service levels are possibly not up to the standard they would wish.

This can cause delays in taking up title deeds, issuing contracts, replying to queries and closing sales. So ask your solicitor, when you appoint them, if they have the time to deal with your sale. It's a simple question, but hold them to what you would deem to be a professional level of service.

CHECKLIST

These are papers your solicitor will need from you to work on the legal aspects of the sale of your property:

1. Your deeds or a letter of authority signed by you, quoting your mortgage reference number, addressed to your lending institution and authority to take up your deeds.

2. Your and your partner's PPS numbers.

3. If married, your state marriage certificate (your church marriage certificate is not sufficient).

4. If separated or divorced, the separation agreement or court order.

5. Up-to-date receipts of any local-authority charges.

6. Up-to-date ground-rent receipts (if applicable).

7. Copy of planning permission and architect's certificate of compliance for your property.

8. Certificate of exemption (if applicable) for any alterations carried out to the property.

9. Details of all services connected to the

property (gas, electricity, etc.). In the case of sales of apartments, there are additional requirements regarding the management-company accounts and service charges. Your solicitor should let you have a detailed list of these requirements once you instruct them to act for you.

CHAPTER 11

APARTMENTS AND MANAGEMENT COMPANIES

Selling an apartment is different from selling a house. Purchasers of an apartment are not only buying your home but are also buying into the management company that controls the whole complex. This includes the grounds, the common areas, car-parking, the lifts and all that these entail.

Apartments in well-run and -managed complexes are infinitely easier to sell and do so for a better price than those in equivalently located developments which are poorly managed. If you are an apartment owner, you are normally a member of the management company, with ownership on the basis on one share per apartment. The management company is responsible for the maintenance of the common areas, both internal and external. An efficient managing agent will ensure that the appearance of the development is maintained and is not allowed to fall into a state of disrepair that could have a detrimental effect on the value of your property.

Once an interested party has seen and bid on your apartment, there are a lot of documents and enquiries required behind the scenes to enable the transaction to run smoothly.

First, ensure that you have up-to-date contact numbers for the managing agents, as potential purchasers will want these. Also, have a copy of the rules of your management company available to show to prospective purchasers.

A copy of the current year's service charge budget will also be needed. This should include the present level of the sinking fund, as savvy purchasers will wish to ensure that there are sufficient funds in place to cover the cost of repairs and other expenditure for the forthcoming years. It should also detail the major repairs or investments due to be carried out in the near future.

If you live in a development with a number of separate blocks, it is a good idea to nominate representatives in each block to liaise with the managing agents on day-to-day issues. Inform potential purchasers if this has been done in your complex.

It is important for you to keep fully informed about the running of the management company and to take an active role in it while living in the apartment. It will also help your sale to proceed smoothly if you are in a position to answer the above queries in an efficient and speedy manner. You have the right to attend the annual general meeting of the management company and to vote in relation to the running of your apartment complex. You should do so.

When you are selling your apartment, your solicitor will need the following documents and information from you, or the managing agent.

- A certified copy of the certificate of incorporation and memorandum and articles of association of the management company.
- Evidence by way of a Companies Office search that the management company is still registered with the Companies Office. (This is because many management companies have been struck off due to non-filing of annual accounts.)
- A copy of the folio showing the management company as registered owner or a copy of the deed of assurance of reversionary interest to the management company.

- A certified copy of the block insurance policy. The name of the purchaser and, if requested, the interest of the mortgagee must be noted thereon before completion and evidence by letter from the insurance company confirming that it will not cancel, lapse or fail to renew the policy without first giving fifteen days notice prior to cancellation to the purchaser/mortgage provider.
- If the management company is not the owner of the reversionary interest, a copy of the contract for sale of the reversionary interest to the management company.
- Confirmation as to when it is anticipated the sale to the management company will be completed.
- Evidence that the developer, if still involved in the development, is still registered with the Companies Office.

Your solicitor will have to undertake to confirm that one management company is or will be responsible for management of the external and/or internal common areas of the entire development and all services relating to it.

WHO IS MANAGING THE COMPLEX?

If a firm of managing agents have been engaged, the

following information will need to be supplied to the purchasers' solicitor:

- The name of the firm (managing the complex).
- The terms of their engagement including (in particular) the amount of their charges.
- Whether they are employed by the developer or the management company.
- Confirmation that the only shareholders in the management company are the unit owners.
- Share certificate in or certificate of membership of the management company in the name of the vendor.
- Share transfer form duly completed by vendor (where applicable).
- Confirmation that each of the unit owners has or will have equal shareholdings or voting rights.
- Confirmation that the service charge is or will be divided equally amongst the number of units in the development (this is often done on the basis of apartment size, or number of bedrooms).
- Confirmation that no persons other than unit owners (in particular the developer or its nominees) will hold shares or voting rights in the management company.
- Receipt for the latest payment of the service charges.

They will also need to ascertain if the management company is aware of any possible claim against the company's funds or of any proposal by the company to carry out any repair work or incur other expenditure which would substantially affect the annual service charge payable at present. This could range from a compensation claim regarding an accident in the common area to work planned for the future.

Solicitors will perform additional checks for tax-designated properties. We do not examine these here as they are of a very technical nature.

Finally, if you agreed to become a director or company secretary of the management company, ensure that you resign once you sell your unit.

As you can see, there is extra paperwork involved for you and your solicitor if you are selling an apartment as opposed to a conventional house. By being efficient and attending the annual general meetings of your management company, you will be able to provide much of the information to prospective buyers and thereby assist your sale to run smoothly.

CHAPTER 12

TROUBLESHOOTING

Many home sales progress smoothly through the sales process. You, the owner, move from appointing an estate agent (or not) to the showing of the property and moving to 'sale agreed' and 'sold' in a relatively seamless manner. The sale closes as expected, and you receive your money with little hassle.

But no two sales work out exactly the same. Some are a dream: you place your property, a buyer comes along, they offer you a good price, you accept, and contracts get signed promptly. Other sales can be a different story. Delays and problems occur from day one. It is only by facing up to these problems that your sale can proceed. This chapter deals with a few of the problems that can cause delays to a sale. Many of the reasons for delays have been covered already, and most can be avoided by appointing the correct professionals to assist you in the first place.

Some properties have an interesting sales process. A few years ago in Cork, a middle-aged German woman experienced one particularly interesting reason why a house might not sell. She had bought a beautiful holiday home in a tranquil village in the late 1980s but found that by the early part of the new millennium she was not visiting it often and so decided to sell. She gave the sale of her property to a local agent, one she knew socially, after what was scheduled to be her last summer in the house. (She never visited in the winter as she was an avid skier.)

After nine months of having her holiday home on the market and continuously reading in the press and on the Internet that it was a very buoyant time for all types of property in Ireland (even the German newspapers reported on the strength of the Celtic economy and its property prices), she began to get concerned. She had received no offers on her home; almost every time she rang her auctioneer's office, he was out; and the office staff would say on most occasions that he was showing her property. Why had she not received any offers?

As her agent was not returning telephone calls and didn't seem to believe in e-mails, she decided to make a surprise visit to West Cork to meet him. She arrived at her estate agent's office to be told again that he was out showing her property. She decided to go immediately to the property and meet him there.

When she arrived, she found out why her property wasn't selling. The agent was there all right, but he wasn't exactly focusing much attention on showing the property. Let's just say he was partially clothed and so was his female companion. It transpired that he was having 'marital difficulties' and that his new partner was living rent-free in the German lady's property since soon after the time she had last visited the property and returned to Germany.

Needless to say, the property was given to another, more professional, auctioneer immediately and was 'sale agreed' within a few weeks. According to the German woman, the first agent paid very dearly for her relative silence: the story soon became public, as all Irish towns have small business communities, and some secrets are very hard to keep.

SALE IS SLOW TO COMPLETE

There can be many reasons for a sale being slow to complete. Once the estate agent has introduced the buyer and instructed your solicitor, the primary responsibility for ensuring that there is no major delay, from then to completion, rests with your solicitor.

If your buyer has not signed the contract, it may be that the contract for the sale of your home is on an unconditional basis (that is, it is not subject to the sale of another property) but that the purchaser is nevertheless awaiting the execution of contracts on their own property before signing your contract. If this is the case, you must decide, in consultation with your estate agent and solicitor, how much time you will permit before you withdraw the contract and seek another buyer.

Stay in regular touch with your solicitor. If delays ensue and your solicitor cannot ascertain their cause, ask your estate agent to see what they can do to expedite matters or, at the very least, to discover the reason for the delay.

THE ENGINEER'S REPORT

Most sales are subject to the purchaser being happy with an engineer's report on your property. Even if the purchaser says that they do not require one, their solicitor or bank will often insist that one is done. There is no pass or fail mark with engineers' reports. All houses have cracks and possible problems. Discuss any problems with the prospective purchaser that arise as a result of the engineer's report . They can't expect everything to be perfect, and small problems should not affect your sale.

Should there be a major problem with your property, get an engineer's report yourself and see if any problems are covered by your home insurance. You may need to consider getting the work done in order to get the best price for your home.

The main point to note about an engineer's report is that the purchaser normally requires this before they can sign contracts, so ensure that they do it within a few days of agreeing the sale.

Prospective purchasers are terrified of the word 'subsidence'. Once the word is mentioned, even if it is only one of a number of possibilities given by an engineer too lazy to investigate the true source of a crack, most purchasers get scared. Do they not look around their own home, lodgings or current rental accommodation and see the cracks? 'Ah, they're fine, they've been there since I was small' is invariably the answer. The same is probably true for the home they are considering buying.

I have my suspicions about the epidemic of subsidence that has swept many parts of suburban Ireland over the past ten years. People see a crack and assume that the house is subsiding. In the vast majority of cases, this is not so. Cracks in homes can be mere plaster cracks, caused by shrinkage after plastering. They can also be the result of settlement. Settlement is, as the word suggests, where the building or foundation has moved slightly since its construction. This is not a problem – unless the property continues to move. If so, one has a different problem – bad foundations or subsidence.

In most older home-insurance policies, subsidence is covered, but settlement, bad drains, etc., are not normally covered. Therefore, many vested interests have come together – the homeowner's engineers, the 'subsidence specialist' builders and solicitors – to classify any fault as subsidence and so line the pockets of 'subsidence specialists', who normally do no more than pour loads of concrete, and sometimes steel, under the foundations of a home. Naturally, drains, which may have been the main problem, will have to be replaced, and some replastering and decorating will have to be done to the house also.

SUDDEN DEATH
BEFORE SALE CLOSES

It has been known for the purchaser to die after signing contracts, but before the sale closes. It happened to a couple who bought a house off me a few years ago. They were a young couple, recently engaged. They signed unconditional contracts to buy a second-hand house. The contracts, along with the balance of 10 per cent, were returned to the seller's solicitor, and a closing date was set. The man was killed the following weekend in a car-versus-motorbike crash.

What happened next? As luck would have it, the purchasers had signed up for their mortgage protection/life insurance, and the insurance company paid up. This allowed the man's partner to proceed with the deal and purchase the house, mortgage free. A very sad situation, but, from our seller's point of view, their sale proceeded. The purchaser sold the house soon after as, emotionally, she could not settle there – after all, it was to be their home together.

More recently, in a development of new homes, a prospective purchaser died after signing contracts. He was an investor and was not bothered with life insurance. Legally, the builder could have (1) kept the 15 per cent already paid and sued the estate for the balance of the purchase price; (2) kept the 15 per cent if the estate did not proceed with the purchase. Sense and common decency prevailed, as, in fairness, it normally does. The builder refunded the 15 per cent to the estate immediately and proceeded to resell the property.

Ensure that your purchaser has life insurance/mortgage protection in place, just in case. Then, get your solicitor to close the sale as soon as possible, before anybody can die, lose their job, split up, get injured or any other calamity that might affect your sale. They all happen, and having contracts signed is no real good if the purchaser can't get the mortgage to pay the balance.

A CHANGE OF MIND

Sometimes, the purchaser signs and returns contracts and then changes their mind. This is very unusual, but unusual things happen when property is involved. You basically have two options. The first option is to leave the purchaser, who has signed the contract, and back out of the deal. You are fully entitled to keep their 10 per cent deposit, as they have caused you considerable inconvenience.

The second option is to get your solicitor to sue them to force them to close. Before you go down this route, it is highly advisable to get your solicitor to speak to the purchaser's solicitor to ascertain why they are no longer proceeding. It could well be that they can't proceed. Reasons for this could include job loss or accident. If they just can't complete the purchase, there is no practical point in pursuing them. In cases where the purchaser just couldn't complete due to unfortunate circumstances, I have seen builders refund the full deposit. Few people want to kick somebody when they are down.

If they just won't complete the purchase because they have changed their mind, that's a different story. Unfortunately, after signing a contract, they are legally bound to proceed or pay penalties. Otherwise, there would be no point in having contracts. Talk over with your solicitor whether you should sue them to force them to complete (this could take a long time) or whether to just keep their 10 per cent deposit and sell the property again.

I once dealt with an individual who, after signing unconditional contracts, changed his mind. He had found a cheaper property elsewhere. When it became clear that he would lose the deposit paid to me as auctioneer for the vendor, along with the balance of the 10 per cent he paid to his solicitor, which was forwarded to the solicitor on the other side, he proceeded with the purchase. He would have lost about €25,000 if he had backed out. The scary part of that story is that the individual involved was a chef working four doors down the road, and he arrived into my office in full chef gear – hat, apron and knives – looking for, nay *demanding*, his deposit back. When a colleague rang the Gardaí, he apologised and said that as he had left work in a hurry he didn't realise he still had one of his kitchen knives in his hand . . . and some people think that auctioneering is an easy life!

GAZUMPING

Your agent is duty-bound to disclose a higher offer to you, the vendor, even if it has been received after a sale has been agreed or a deposit has been taken on your property. If you, as a seller, accept the higher offer after verbally agreeing to sell your property to someone else, this is called gazumping. Some buyers also withdraw from agreed purchases, for no good reason, or place deposits on more than one property at a time, leaving you, the vendor, gazundered.

Gazumping may happen at any stage up until you sign the formal contract. Until then, you are not contractually bound to the deal. So, it is not a problem for you to worry about when you are selling. If anything, it is a major plus. Until you sign the contract, you can accept higher offers.

While purchasers see it as reneging on a deal, and it is, many buyers correctly do not view themselves as bound to purchase simply because they pay a booking deposit. It is slightly odd, therefore, for them to conclude that the vendor is unilaterally bound to the deal.

Many vendors will continue with the sale that they had agreed (after all, where were these new bidders when the property was actively on the market), though some people will accept a higher offer unless they are contractually bound to proceed with the sale. The decision is yours.

While gazumping has received adverse publicity, most people would be tempted to accept a bid of an extra few thousand euro for their property. (See Chapter 9 for some advice on how to decide which offer to accept.)

When gazumping takes place, estate agents are merely the bearers of bad tidings to the jilted party (or, alternatively, of good tidings to those on the right side of the equation). Gazumping is the action of sellers and not auctioneers. Normally a party becomes contractually committed once he or she signs the formal contract in respect of the sale. Up to that point, an estate agent is legally obliged to disclose all offers received for the property to the seller.

The law in this country allows, and even encourages, gazumping. Many, many suggestions for changes have been made over the years by property commentators, politicians and letter-writers to newspapers, but the law has stayed the same. One simple solution, which could be speedily put in place, and which would mirror the practices of some of our European neighbours, is as follows.

When a sale is agreed, the purchaser should place a deposit on the property (as is done at present). If, for any reason, the seller backs out of the deal, they (the seller) have to pay compensation to the scorned potential purchaser of a sum equal to or even double the value of the deposit. Deposits on most second-hand homes are €5,000, €10,000 or even €20,000. Sellers will not pull out of deals lightly when it costs them money. Gazumping will disappear overnight, as the financial incentive to accept a slightly higher offer will no longer exist, unless, of course, the new offer is significantly more than the deposit placed on the property.

Until then, there will always be an incentive for buyers or sellers to renege on a deal and to go with a more advantageous offer. As a seller, gazumping is a nice problem; it means that you have a higher offer on your property. Just be careful that the bidders are genuine before you accept. I have seen many a seller accept a gazumping offer, only to have a new potential purchaser back out at the last minute, leaving the seller with no sale. It's hard to feel sorry for them.

THE HARD-TO-SELL HOME

The quickest way to move a hard-to-sell home is to reduce the price. This is easy to do, and effective, but it is expensive. Before reducing the price, you might consider the following: Did you choose the wrong estate agent? Did you go with the agent who gave you the highest and most overly optimistic valuation on your home? If so, consider using one of the other agents who were more honest with you on price. Don't reward the agent who made a fool of you.

Appoint a poor agent to represent you at your peril. A thousand euro saved on fees can be the worst 'investment' you ever make. The same is true for your solicitor. Make sure to appoint one who will do their job efficiently and professionally.

CHAPTER 13

TERMS INVOLVED IN THE SALES PROCESS

Communication is important in all walks of life, especially in stressful times. When selling your home, it is important to have a strong grasp of the meaning of words and terms used by the professionals you meet during the course of your sale. These professionals include your solicitor, estate agent, engineer, banker or mortgage broker and mortgage valuer.

An understanding of these terms will allow you to fully participate in the sales process for your home from a position of strength, confident in the knowledge that you know what is happening at each and every stage of the process.

100 per cent mortgage A mortgage loan in which the borrower receives a loan amount equivalent to the total value of the property to be purchased. In this situation, the borrower does not need to use any savings, etc., to secure the loan.

advance The amount of a loan received by the borrower, from a bank or other financial institution. This can also be called the principal or capital sum.

agency A term used to describe the relationship between the property-seller and their auctioneer. Agency terms and fees should be detailed in writing.

annualised percentage rate (APR) This is a financial tool to help you identify the true cost of borrowing. It gives you a way of comparing the true cost of different types of loans, from different lenders, on an annual basis. It evaluates the rate, the way it is applied daily, weekly, monthly and any other fees and charges involved.

annuity mortgage This is another name for a standard capital and interest repayment mortgage.

architect's certificate This is required for any property constructed since the Planning Acts came into force in 1964. An architect's certificate legally certifies that the conditions attached to the grant of planning permission have been complied with.

assignment The transfer of ownership from the current owner of a property to another is called an assignment. It is a term used by solicitors. Property, insurance policies or property leases are all items that can be assigned.

auctioneer Also called valuer or estate agent. This term is used to describe individuals or companies licensed to sell property in Ireland. Ensure your auctioneer is qualified and licensed, i.e., a member of the IAVI or the IPAV.

bridging finance This is a relatively short-term loan which you take out when you have bought or built a property without first selling the one you already/previously own. A bridging loan is normally paid off upon sale of the first property. There are a few problems with bridging loans. First, they are extremely hard to get. Many financial institutions will only give you bridging finance once you have unconditional contracts signed on the house you are selling. Otherwise, the banks often judge your eligibility based on your capacity to make repayments on both mortgages over the full lifetime of a mortgage. While you fully intend to sell the first house as fast as possible, the bank assumes that it will never be sold. Bridging finance is much more expensive than a standard mortgage. Banks seem to work off a margin of up to 2 full percentage points above their standard mortgage rate. There are two types of bridging finance: open- and close-ended bridging. Open-ended bridging finance is when the contracts for the sale of your original property are not yet signed. It may be that your property is not yet sale agreed or even on the market. Close-ended bridging is when you have sale agreed your first home, contracts are signed, and a closing date has been set. A difference in closing dates exists but is defined. The bank knows how long the bridging loan is for.

building regulations Building regulations deal with such issues as building standards, workmanship, conservation of fuel and energy and access for people with disabilities. They are constantly under review and upgrade the standard of construction continuously. Full details of the current building regulations can be found at the Department of the Environment website, www.environ.ie.

chain of title This details the lineage of the ownership of a property. It details the names and rights of past owners of a property, when the title was transferred from them and to whom.

closing This is when you pay the balance of the purchase price and in return receive the keys to the house or property.

commercial property Commercial property is solely used for business purposes. Examples are shops, industrial units, petrol stations, convenience stores and offices.

completion *See* closing.

contracts These are the documents which set out all the details of the transaction for the transfer of the ownership of the house. These will be drawn up by the solicitor for the seller.

conveyancing This is the term used by solicitors to describe the legal process for transferring the title and ownership of property and land, from one party to another.

credit report A lender will decide whether to give a loan based on information contained on your application form and on your credit report. A credit report lists all of your borrowings and any late payments or defaults on payments that have been reported by members of the Credit Bureau. The Credit Bureau in Ireland includes all the main lending institutions.

deposit A deposit is the initial down payment for a house. This is payable to the agent of the seller of the property, usually an auctioneer. It will normally be in the region of 3–5 per cent of the agreed purchase price. A receipt should be requested, and all deposits should be given only to bonded auctioneers.

disbursements (conveyancing and outlay) This is the amount your solicitor will be charged to carry out their work such as searches, registration fees, photo-copying, postage and couriers. It will be charged to you on top of their quoted fee. They are items that your solicitor pays in order to carry out the convey-ance on your behalf.

estate agent *See* auctioneer.

European Central Bank (ECB) The ECB sets interest rates for all the countries within the euro zone. Mort-gage rates are normally between 0.5 per cent and 2 per cent higher than the ECB rate.

encumbrance This is a claim, loan or judgement reg-istered against the title of a property. It hinders a sel-ler's ability to pass good title to a purchaser. If there is an encumbrance on a property you are buying or sell-ing, the seller's solicitor will need to give an undertak-ing to discharge the same upon closing the sale.

family home (statutory) declaration This is a sworn statement. It clarifies the ownership of the house and declares whether it was used as a family home or not. In the case of marriage separation/divorce, sections of the separation/divorce agreement would need to be produced.

fixtures Fixtures include furniture such as built-in wardrobes, kitchen presses, bookcases, recessed lights, etc. They are items that are permanently attached to the property and, therefore, legally included in the sale. If in doubt on whether something is a fixture or not, advice should be sought from your solicitor.

freehold This means that the owner of a property also owns the land it is built upon and all that land around it outlined in the plan deposited with the Land Registry.

gazump This means raising the price of a property to a higher price than previously verbally agreed – basically raising the price before the contracts are signed and the deal is legally binding.

gazunder This occurs when a buyer reduces his or her bid for a property before the deal has been signed and finalised. A buyer might offer less because he or she knows that the seller desperately wants to sell the property.

ground rent An annual charge made to the owner of the freehold of a leasehold property. Ground rents are normally for nominal amounts. One usually has the right to buy the freehold title.

homebond This is a service provided by the National

Housing Building Guarantee Scheme, through registered builders, to people buying new, privately built houses and apartments. The actual certificate is called the 'HB47'. It provides:

- a guarantee against losing your deposit if the builder goes bankrupt or into liquidation;
- a ten-year defect warranty against major structural faults that happen within ten years of completion.

All new homes should have either a 'homebond' or a 'premier bond' guarantee.

housing starts The number of residential building construction projects that have begun during any particular month or year. This is considered to be a crucial indicator of the strength of both the economy and the construction sector. If the economy is strong, people are more likely to buy new homes, and, consequently, the number of housing starts is high. Ireland is currently producing in the region of 90,000 new homes per year.

insurances There are three main types of insurances associated with a mortgage and a property purchase.

1. **life assurance**: This is compulsory if you are taking out a residential mortgage. There are two main types of life assurance:

(a) mortgage protection: This means the amount outstanding on your home loan will be repaid in the event of your death. The amount that is to be paid out reduces in line with your mortgage over the years.

(b) term assurance: This is life assurance that does not reduce during the term of the loan. In the event of death, the mortgage is repaid and the surplus of the money goes into the estate of the deceased.

2. **house insurance**: This is compulsory for those taking out a mortgage. This insures you against damage to your home, up to and including the rebuilding of your home should it be destroyed, by fire, flood or any other means.

3. **mortgage payment protection**: This form of insurance is not compulsory. If you cannot work because of an accident, illness or because you have been made redundant, this policy will cover the repayments on your mortgage (and more if you wish) for a period of time, usually up to twelve months.

interest This is simply the cost of borrowing money. Interest rates can be:

1. *fixed*: A loan where the payments are based on a constant interest rate for a set period of

time.

2.. *variable or tracker*: This means that the interest rate charged on the mortgage can go up and down over the term of the mortgage.

3. *interim interest*: As soon as you draw your loan, interest begins to accrue. However, the first mortgage payment normally falls due only on the following month. The interest that accrues between your receiving the money and the first repayment is known as interim interest. This can be paid at the time or added to the loan.

investment property This means property that generates income or is otherwise intended for investment purposes rather than as your primary residence. Common examples of investment properties are apartment buildings and rental houses, in which the owners do not live in the residential units but use them to generate ongoing rental income from tenants. Those who invest in property also expect to generate capital gains as property values increase over time.

land certificate A certificate issued by the Land Registry confirming the ownership of a property.

land registry fee This is the fee paid to the Land Registry Office to update their records with you as the new owner of the property after you buy your home. This fee will be included in the legal costs charged by your solicitor. (*See* disbursements.)

leasehold A person buying a leasehold property does not own the land upon which the house is built and pays an annual rent for the privilege of doing so. This is called ground rent. Most leaseholders have the right to purchase the freehold title to the property and should do so.

lessee The person who rents land or a property from the owner (a lessor). The lessee is also known as the tenant. Always read your lease agreement carefully, it is a legally binding document.

lessor The person who rents land or property to a lessee. The lessor is also known as the 'landlord'.

life assurance Life assurance is normally required by the lending institution, when lending against a family home. It provides added security for the lender. They do not want to have to evict a grieving widow or widower from the family home, because the wage earning party has died and the surviving spouse is not in a position to earn enough to keep up payments. In the case of a property bought as an investment, life assurance is often not required as the bank has an alternative source of comfort – the income that the property generates in the form of rent. If the investor dies, rents continue to be paid.

listing A term used by auctioneers, valuers and estate agents to signify that they have the rights to sell a certain property.

loan application fee This may be charged by your bank or mortgage broker for processing your mortgage application. In the current competitive environment, this fee will usually be waived.

loan to value (LTV) The amount you wish to borrow expressed as a percentage of the value of the property you are using as security, i.e., a loan of €300,000 on a property valued at €400,000 has a 75 per cent LTV.

money-laundering Money-laundering is the way in which criminals attempt to turn cash and assets obtained from criminal activities into genuine assets through the financial system. In Ireland, money-laundering has been treated as a very serious offence since the passing of the Criminal Justice Act 1994.

mortgage A mortgage is the amount of money lent by a financial institution for a specified term of years to buy a property.

mortgage broker An individual or company that introduces mortgage business to a bank or building society. They are registered and regulated by the Irish Financial Services Regulatory Authority and are paid by the financial institutions.

mortgage indemnity bond A type of insurance that covers the financial institution in the event that they make a loss on the sale of a repossessed property. It normally comes into effect when the loan amount exceeds 75 per cent of the purchase price or property value. Again, in this competitive environment, this fee will normally be waived, if requested.

mortgage redemption This is the amount of money still to be paid to your financial institution, the remainder of the loan for the property being sold. This will normally be paid from the proceeds of the sale of your property by your solicitor and is usually a condition imposed by the lender for releasing the deeds to your solicitor.

open house An American term to describe when the estate agent advertises that a house may be viewed during set times.

open market value The price a ready, willing and able buyer will agree to pay to a willing seller in the current market.

power of attorney The legal power granted to another to act on your behalf. Sometimes purchasers or sellers grant a power of attorney to their solicitor or family member to act on their behalf if they cannot be present.

premier guarantee This is a ten-year structural-defects policy for residential and commercial developments. Most new homes are covered by either a home-bond or premier guarantee.

principal private residence The primary location in which a person resides. It is where you live most of the time. There is no capital-gains tax on the sale of your principal private residence.

probate sale A term used to describe the sale of a property where the owner has passed away. This is also called an executor's sale as it is the executor of the will who is selling on behalf of the deceased person's estate.

registration of title The title deeds are registered in the Registry of Deeds or in the Land Registry. The cost of this will be included in your outlays from your solicitor. (*See* disbursements.)

retention An amount of a mortgage withheld by the lender while repairs, which the property valuer has specified, are carried out on the property. The amount of the retention, if any, is usually recommended by the valuer.

retention (planning permission) This is where a person has already carried out a development without getting the necessary planning consents and now wants to regulate the situation by getting planning permission to retain the development. In a residential scenario, it could apply to garage or attic conversions or extensions to the property.

reserve price This is a term used when a property is being sold at auction. Once the reserve price has been reached, and this is announced, the property will then be sold to the highest bidder.

searches These will be carried out on the day the transaction is due to be completed. They will determine whether any judgements have been registered on the property or against the sellers. It will also indicate whether there are any planning restrictions or planning changes. The searches are carried out by a firm of law searchers under the instruction of your solicitor. Searches are not done until the day of closing to ensure that the property you are purchasing is free of judgement.

security/collateral The mortgage is secured against your home. A lender is entitled to sell the house if you do not make the necessary repayments. The property is their security or collateral.

stamp duty This is a tax paid to the Government when you purchase a property. Stamp-duty rates change regularly (at budget time). They currently range from 0 to 9 per cent of the full price, depending on the property's value and your circumstances. (See Appendix B for the latest stamp-duty rates.)

stamp duty on mortgages Another hidden tax! This tax is currently calculated on mortgages greater than €254,000.

subject to contract Most letters regarding the sale of property include the words 'Subject to Contract/Contract Denied'. This means that until a legally binding contract is prepared by the seller's solicitor and is signed by both the purchaser and the vendor, no binding agreement is deemed to be in existence.

structural survey An inspection of the property to check that it is structurally sound. Ensure that your engineer is qualified and that they will write their report in plain English and not engineer-speak.

title This refers to the ownership of a particular piece of property.

title deeds These are the documents of ownership to the property. They are retained by the lender as security for the loan until it is paid in full.

tracker mortgages Tracker mortgages are set at a certain fixed percentage above the ECB rate.

valuation An inspection, carried out by a qualified valuer. It is carried out on behalf of your mortgage lender to see if the property you are buying will provide good security for the loan they are going to advance to you. This is not a structural survey and should not be confused with it.

valuer *See* auctioneer.

vendor The seller.

zoning Government (local government, i.e., county council or town council) laws that control the use of land within a jurisdiction. Zoning areas may be classified as residential, commercial, farming and so on.

CHAPTER 14

COMPLETING THE SALE
AND MOVING ON

Finally, the day your sale is closing arrives. We have already discussed the legal aspects. Now we will look at what exactly happens on what can be an emotional day as you move out of what was your home. This is the also the day that you get your hands on the sales proceeds. At this point, 99 per cent of your work is done.

CLOSING AND
COLLECTING YOUR MONEY

The final step in selling your home is referred to as 'closing'. Once you have found a buyer and have received unconditional contracts for the sale of your home, it takes only a few weeks to 'close' the sale. By this, we mean the actual point at which you transfer the ownership, possession and title of the home over to the new buyer and you receive the selling price for your house.

MOVING OUT

Contracts have been signed and exchanged, and your solicitor has arranged the closing date, normally a few weeks away. Don't panic: we will now discuss what you need to do.

As soon as a closing date has been agreed, you should contact your utility providers (gas, phone, power, cable television, etc.). Advise them of your final billing date and also instruct them to set up accounts for your new home, whether you have purchased, built or are renting.

Send out change-of-address cards to friends, family and relatives by post or by e-mail. Contact the post office to get your mail forwarded. You will need to do this at least five days before you want the service to begin. Remember to leave a forwarding address with the owners of your old house. Who knows, they might be able to forward a gift from a forgetful relative or a prize-bond win. Here is a comprehensive list of tasks, people and services who need to be informed of your move.

1. Re-direct post and send change-of-address cards.
2. Transfer utilities: gas, electricity and waste collection.
3. Telephone, including mobile, broadband and line rental.
4. Television licence.
5. Cable/digital television company.
6. Electoral register.
7. Driving licence, car insurance, vehicle registration details.
8. Insurance: house, health and life insurance.
9. Banks, building societies and credit-card companies.
10. The Revenue Commissioners.
11. Social insurance and social-security payments.
12. Health professionals (doctor, dentist, etc.).
13. Schools and places of employment.
14. Publications and subscriptions.
15. Trade unions, professional bodies and clubs/societies.
16. Other licences: dog, fishing, etc.

Don't forget to organise the removal van or friends to help on moving day. Before committing to a commercial mover, be sure to get at least three estimates. Find out what their insurance policy covers. Usually, the movers must be paid in cash.

Now is a good time to weed out things you no longer use. As mentioned earlier, the recycling centre and local dump are your friends.

The sooner you start collecting packing materials and packing up, the better. Pack the things that you rarely use first. Only move what you feel you will use in your new home. Be sure to label boxes with their contents and where they are to go in the new house. For your own sake, don't pack boxes with too many heavy items. They might break or, alternatively, your back might.

Most furniture comes apart, and there will be less damage both to your furniture, and to both houses, if you remove legs, doors, etc., where possible.

Pack your DIY tools where you can find easily them. You are bound to need a screwdriver or other tools as soon as you move in. If they have been packed away at the bottom of a large box, you will only go mad looking for them.

BE NICE

Do leave the house in good order. Many buyers ask to see the property on the morning that the sale is closing. They want to be sure that it is in the same condition as when they viewed it. They will also want to ensure that no damage has been done while you were moving out.

Have the grass cut and leave the garden in good shape. Don't dig up and remove the rose bushes (somebody did that to me) or any other plants from the garden. Try not to leave rubbish out for the new owners to dump.

Sometimes you will meet the purchasers of your new home. If the sales process went smoothly, you might want to spend a few minutes with them and wish them well in their new home. You might be able to show them how the heating or the immersion works.

One of the kindest gestures I have seen is when the seller leaves out a few cups, teabags, milk and a kettle for the purchasers. It is only a cup of tea, but after a hard and stressful day, which they are certain to have had, it will be much appreciated.

APPENDIX A

SAMPLE LETTER OF APPOINTMENT

This sample letter of appointment is printed courtesy of the IAVI. Its general format is utilised by many auctioneering firms, with some minor variations. It is printed here to give readers an idea of the type of letter and standard conditions involved in a client–agency relationship such as a house vendor and their auctioneer.

[*Vendor(s) address*]

Re: Proposed sale of [*address of subject property*]

Dear [*Vendor's name*]

I write to thank you for instructing [*name of auctioneering firm*] in respect of the proposed sale of the above property and, as required by regulations governing this firm, I wish to confirm the following arrangements.

AGENCY

You have appointed [*name of auctioneering firm*] as sole agent, and you will be liable to this firm for a fee on the agreed basis set out below if a ready, willing and able purchaser is introduced:

> 1. by any agency at a price accepted by you during the period of this sole agency; or,
>
> 2. if unconditional contracts for the sale of the property are exchanged, after the expiry of this sole agency, with a purchaser

(a) who was introduced during the period of this sole agency by any agent; or,

(b) with whom [*name of auctioneering firm*] or any sub-agent had negotiations about the property; or,

(c) who received particulars of the property during the period of this sole agency from, or who otherwise enquired about the property to [*name of auctioneering firm*].

Duration of agency

This sole agency has been agreed for a period of three calendar months [*adjust as necessary*] from today's date, subject to the right of either party to terminate the contract on giving one week's written notice. Termination of the contract will not negate your liability to us for fees, if they arise based on this contract, and outlay.

FEES

In any of the circumstances described under 'Agency' above, you will be liable to us for our professional fees, which are agreed at __ per cent of both the contract price and the value of any items forming part of the consideration between the parties, including fixtures and fittings. VAT on such fees, at the appropriate rate – currently 21 per cent – is also payable by you.

OUTLAY

You will be further liable for outlay incurred by this firm on your behalf during the period of this sole agency, to an agreed limit of €_____ , together with VAT thereon at the appropriate rate, currently 21 per cent. Of this outlay, approximately €_____ will be spent on advertising in the following newspapers: [*names of newspapers*], €_____ on internet listings and the balance on the preparation and distribution of a sales brochure, including photography, signage erected and removed from the property, auction-room hire and other incidental but direct costs. This outlay budget will not be exceeded without such an increase being agreed between us and confirmed in writing to you.

DEPOSIT

You authorise [*name of auctioneering firm*] to secure an initial deposit of 5 per cent of the sale price in the event of a sale being agreed and to offset this amount against sums due to us under this contract of agency on the closing of the sale.

BROCHURE

We enclose a draft brochure in respect of the subject property, which we would propose to issue to the public. We ask that you examine this draft brochure for accuracy and/or omissions. In the event that you do not revert in writing with suggested amendments within the next seven days, it will be presumed that you confirm that the particulars set forth are accurate.

[*The following wording is an example of the type of caveat that may be inserted but obviously the detail will vary with each property.*]

In particular, we draw your attention to the fact that you have assured us that an architect's certificate of compliance with building regulations exists in relation to the rear ground-floor extension. We have not had sight of this certificate and will proceed on the basis of your assurance, but we request that the certificate be provided to us as soon as possible by your solicitor.

INCLUSIONS

[*The following is an example of wording that might be used – amend as appropriate.*]

You have instructed us that the following are to be specifically included in the sale: all fitted carpets and curtains; the light fittings in all rooms with the exception of the chandelier in the lounge which you will replace with a standard fitting prior to the sale closing (our brochure will note this fact) and both the Belling electric cooker and Philips fridge-freezer in the kitchen.

VIEWINGS

The property will be on view by prior appointment at times agreed with you in advance/on public view on _____days and _____days from __pm until __pm [*delete as appropriate*]. We confirm receipt of a set of keys to facilitate these viewings/We would ask that you arrange to provide us with a set of keys to facilitate these viewings [*delete as appropriate*]. You are strongly advised to ensure that all valuables, particularly small valuables, are removed from the property during viewings.

All callers in respect of the property must be referred to us so that we may be best positioned to properly advise you and maximise your return from the proposed sale.

ASKING PRICE AND SALE METHOD

In accordance with the rules of our professional body, the IAVI, we advise you that in our view the value of this property (termed the advised minimum value, AMV) is in the order of €_____. While this represents our true opinion of value prior to marketing commencing, you are advised that it is not a formal valuation and that you must not rely on this price being secured in the market. At the end of the day, the price obtained for the subject property will depend on competition between buyers, and no one can predict with total accuracy what price any property will fetch until a sale is effected. You must not, therefore, rely on this figure in advance of a sale in respect of another property purchase or for any other reason.

Should the AMV turn out to be the sale price, the fee that would become payable to this firm would be €_____ plus VAT on the foregoing agreed basis. However, the fee would be dependent on the actual sale price. As agreed, the property will be offered for sale by private treaty with an asking price of €_____ , and this asking price will not be changed without your prior agreement and the change being confirmed to you in writing. The asking price may not be lower than the AMV.

SOLICITOR

We are forwarding a copy of this letter of confirmation today to the solicitor handling the sale of the property for you, whom we understand to be Mr / Ms [*delete as appropriate*] of [*name of practice*] at _____.
It is important that you contact your solicitor straight away and instruct him/her [*delete as appropriate*] to secure your title deeds so that a contract may be available to issue as soon as a buyer is secured.

TITLE

We will seek confirmation from your solicitor of the title under which the property is held.

MONEY-LAUNDERING LEGISLATION

Under EU and national legislation aimed at preventing money-laundering, all auctioneers and estate agents are legally obliged to secure from their clients evidence of identity (e.g., copy of passport) and place of residence (e.g., recent utility bills) before acting. It is therefore necessary for you to let us have sight of your passport or driver's licence and evidence of address. These documents will be photocopied and the originals returned to you. Alternatively, you may present the originals and pre-prepared photocopies to the agent handling your sale (Mr/Ms [*delete as appropriate*] _____ , who will check the accuracy of the copies and bring the latter to our office.

COMPLAINTS

We are members of Ireland's largest property body, the IAVI, which is based at 38 Merrion Square, Dublin 2. [*Name of auctioneering firm*] has in place an internal complaints procedure in the event that you feel you need to utilise it. This firm is also subject to the rules and regulatory procedures of the IAVI, to whom a complaint may be made independently.

FINANCIAL SERVICES (IF RELEVANT)

[*Name of auctioneering firm*] is an agent for the following institutions and companies and will offer mortgage and/or insurance services to prospective purchasers. However, the tying of the provision of such services to the sale of individual properties is prohibited, and all realistic offers will be treated equally, presented to you for your consideration and noted on our file, as will your response:

[*List lending institutions and insurance companies.*]

Once again, we thank you for your valued instruction and look forward to providing you with a first-rate service. In the event that you do not respond in writing within seven days, you will be deemed to have accepted the foregoing terms, which set out the basis of our agreed contract.

Yours sincerely,

CURRENT STAMP-DUTY RATES

As there are many different rates of stamp duty, depending on the purchaser's situation (first-time buyer, investor, second-time buyer, divorced, etc.) and the use the property is being put to (for own occupation, investment, commercial, etc.), it is important to check the current rates with your solicitor. The Revenue Commissioner also have full details on their website www.revenue.ie. These rates are up to date as of July 2007. Remember that stamp duty applies to the full purchase price, not just the amount over the threshold!

SELLING YOUR HOME

Purchase price €	First-time buyers %	Investor/owner occupier %
0–127,000	0	0
127,000–190,500	0	3
190,501–254,000	0	4
254,001–317,500	0	5
317,501–381,000	0	6
381,001–635,000	0	7.5
635,001–over	0	9